Writing
to
Heal the Soul

Also by the author

Grief Dancers: A Journey into the Depths of the Soul

Writing to Heal the Soul

TRANSFORMING GRIEF
AND LOSS THROUGH WRITING

Susan Zimmermann

THREE RIVERS PRESS
NEW YORK

Grateful acknowledgment is made to the following for permission to reprint previously published material:

Alfred A. Knopf and Walid Nasser & Associates: Excerpts from *The Prophet* by Kahlil Gibran, copyright 1923 and renewed 1951 by Administrators C.T.A. of Kahlil Gibran Estate and Mary G. Gibran. Used by permission of Alfred A. Knopf, a division of Random House, Inc., and Walid Nasser & Associates.

Published by Three Rivers Press, New York, New York.
Member of the Crown Publishing Group.

Random House, Inc. New York, Toronto, London, Sydney, Auckland
www.randomhouse.com

THREE RIVERS PRESS is a registered trademark and the Three Rivers Press colophon is a trademark of Random House, Inc.

Printed in the United States of America

Design by LEONARD HENDERSON

Library of Congress Cataloging-in-Publication Data

Zimmermann, Susan
Writing to heal the soul : transforming grief and loss through
writing / Susan Zimmermann.
p. cm.
Includes bibliographical references.
1. Creative writing—Therapeutic use. 2. Diaries—Therapeutic use. I. Title.

RC489.W75 Z56 2002
616.89'165—dc21
2001034066

ISBN 0-609-80829-X

10 9 8 7 6 5 4 3 2

To

Paul, my love
Katherine, my muse
Helen, my inspiration
Alice, my spice
Mark, my magician
            and
to my amazing grandmothers,
Beatrice and Florine

Acknowledgments

SOMEONE ONCE SAID, "I BELIEVE THAT FRIENDS ARE quiet angels who lift us to our feet when our wings have trouble remembering how to fly." In the writing of this book, many friends have given me a lift. Paul Phillips, my husband and without a doubt the best editor on Earth, has walked each step, holding my hand, and cheering me up on *those* days.

Friends have helped me gather their stories like daffodils in spring, a bud here, blossom there. Their scent wafts throughout these pages: Rosa Venezia, Wendell Fleming, Teri Schwartz, Kate Adams, Betsy Carey, Lucy Buckley, Lorrie Grillo, Leslie White, Nancy Cain, Georgia Heard, Maggie Hudson, Pat Loewi, Ellin Keene, mentors all and brave women whose rough times have never erased their smiles. Rosa Mazone, wise woman, who gave me the gift of perspective. Shelly Espinosa, courageous teacher, who gave me the gift of her experience. Robert Goldhamer, who shared his poetry. James Pennebaker, a stranger, who gave me confidence. Geoffrey and Christy Hoyl, Dave and Joan Braun, Mark Udall, Maggie Fox, and Doug Rovira who led me on adventures that opened new vistas. Donna Bell, whose honesty and goodness have taught me about love.

My children: Katherine, whose silent smile throws wisdom my way; Helen, whose poetry opens doors of truth; Alice, whose laughter makes the house shake; Mark, whose charm chases the blues away. All of them gave me the space to "Keep writing, Mom."

Faye Bender, the most thoughtful, considerate, and persistent agent alive. Betsy Rapoport, my wonderful editor, whose encouragement gave me the faith to "go for it." My mother-in-law, Rita, whose memory continues to bring joy. Paul and Dottie, who have taught me much through their example. And my dear parents and grandparents, who paved the way.

To all of these, my thanks.

Contents

Then a woman said, Speak to us of Joy and Sorrow.
And He answered:
Your joy is your sorrow unmasked.
And the selfsame well from which your
laughter rises was oftentimes filled with your tears.
And how else can it be?
The deeper that sorrow carves into your being,
the more joy you can contain.

And a woman spoke, saying, Tell us of Pain.
And He said:
Your pain is the breaking of the shell
that encloses your understanding.

—From *The Prophet,*
by Kahlil Gibran

Introduction

I became a writer out of desperation, so when I first heard my brother was

dying, I was familiar with the act of saving myself: I would write about him.

—Jamaica Kincaid, *My Brother*

SEVEN YEARS AGO, I ABANDONED A GREAT JOB AND retreated to a converted garage twenty steps from my house to write. I was not a writer. I had no idea where the writing would lead. All I knew was that I had to do it. An inner voice badgered me, insisting that I slow down and reflect. Every morning, when silence engulfed my house, I wrote about my profoundly brain-injured daughter, Katherine, the oldest of my four children, a teenager who functions like a six-month-old.

I wrote because I was confused: I'd been thrown a challenge and didn't know how to deal with it. I'd filled my life with work, children, and other obligations, but had come to realize busyness could be a salve, but not a cure. The pain I felt about Katherine remained, submerged beneath layers of daily distractions. I needed to confront the full scope of what I had lost and somehow keep on. I needed to stop hurting. But I had no idea how. Lasting sorrow, I feared, was my life sentence.

In 1973 I had met Paul. We married during law school at Yale, then moved to Denver where we both worked at downtown firms. Katherine was born five days after my twenty-eighth birthday. It would be an understatement to say I wasn't prepared. I wasn't prepared for the intensity of the love I felt, the purity and completeness of it, the glad surrender to such a tiny creature.

Katherine was perfect at birth. For her first year, she developed normally—rolling over, sitting up, pushing to a stand, saying words on schedule. Around her first birthday, things changed. She started crossing her eyes, wringing her hands, screaming uncontrollably, and retreating into a world we couldn't reach. It was as if my life were an accident in slow motion. I couldn't stop it. I couldn't even scream. Something horrible was happening to one of the people I loved most, and I was utterly helpless.

As Kat's deterioration continued, I began a crazed and fruitless effort to fix her: doctors, diets, therapists. Time passed. Nothing worked. Kat continued her decline.

When Katherine was seven, a physical therapist who had worked with her years before called. She had read an article about Rett syndrome.* It reminded her of Kat. She gave me a phone number. A couple of weeks later, on a gray snowy day, an information packet arrived. I didn't have time to open it until late in the evening after all four children were in bed. When I was in bed myself, I tucked the down comforter around me, opened the packet, and read every word while tears streamed down my face. "God, Paul, I think we finally know what happened to Kat."

The children described *were* Katherine—from the grinding teeth to the blue feet, from the hand-wringing to the curved spines, from the normal beginning to the downward spiral. Katherine's picture was painted on every page. As I read, relief tinged with a piercing despair overwhelmed me. Everything fit. And nothing changed. There was no known cause or cure for Rett

---

*Rett syndrome is a unique neurodevelopmental disorder that is found primarily in females, but that can be seen rarely in males. The disorder results from a mutation in the MECP2 gene on the X chromosome. Prominent features are: apparent normal development until between 6–18 months, followed by a period of regression, which leads to cognitive delay, loss of purposeful hand use and other developmental deficiencies.

syndrome. After so many years, we had a label for Katherine's condition; but Katherine was still Katherine. Her limitations and needs remained the same.

I had a dream around then: I was at a party. People milled around me. Everything seemed festive and upbeat, until I noticed people were staring at me, and I realized with horror that I was different. I was not a person, but a beating heart covered with Band-Aids. The Band-Aids kept falling off.

My heart had not mended, though years had passed. The Band-Aids of three healthy children, a compassionate husband, and meaningful work were not enough. They helped and I was blessed to have them. But the alchemy of sorrow is complicated. A healing environment can provide critical support, but the gut-level change, the transformation from sorrow to acceptance to gratitude, can only come from deep within.

Several busy years passed. At forty, I hit the wall. I couldn't keep going. I quit my job and began to write. Somehow I had to deal with the sadness that sat at my core and grew heavier as I watched Kat enter her teen years, her mind falling ever further behind her changing body. For two years, I lived a hermit's life. When possible, I headed to the Colorado mountains or Utah desert. I sought silence and solitude, things I had never been drawn to. When I wrote, I let my thoughts flow unchecked. Maybe there was a reason that my inner voice had been so merciless. It knew something I didn't: Only through writing could I come to appreciate my life's complex tapestry; only through writing could I get to a place where I embraced my life and everything in it.

A friend gave me *Women Who Run with the Wolves*, in which Clarissa Pinkola Estes retells the medieval tale of "The Handless Maiden." It begins with the devil telling a poor miller that he will never again have to labor at his mill if he will give the devil what stands behind it. Sacrificing the large tree that grows behind the mill seems a small price for freedom from backbreaking labor.

The miller agrees. For a while, the miller and his family prosper. Then one day the devil comes to take what is his. It is the miller's daughter who stands behind the mill.

The devil tries to take the girl, but her innocence repulses him. He orders her not to clean herself for a month. When he returns, she is filthy and bedraggled. He approaches her. She begins to cry. Her tears cleanse her hands. Again the devil is thwarted. Furious, he orders the miller to chop off his daughter's hands and cast her alone into the woods.

After days of hunger, the handless maiden comes upon a splendid orchard. Using the stubs of her arms, she plucks a pear. Unknowingly, she has stolen one of the king's prize pears. The king is outraged until he realizes who the thief is. He takes pity on her, falls in love, marries her, and has a pair of exquisite silver hands made for her. But unlike most "happily ever after" fairy tales, the story doesn't end there. The king goes off to fight his battles, and the handless maiden is much loved in the kingdom. But through the devil's chicanery, the handless maiden—who by then has a child—is once again cast into the woods. Aided by a forest spirit, she makes her way to a small inn where she toils beside the poor innkeepers. As she works, learns, and matures, her hands begin to grow back, evolving over the course of seven years from a baby's hands to the able hands of a woman. Later, when she has made herself whole, she is reunited with her husband.

Estes describes the ordeal in "The Handless Maiden" as a woman's initiation through the rite of endurance. "We don't just go on to go on," she says. "Endurance means we are making something." Only when we go deep into the "forest"—the place deep within where we learn to rely upon ourselves and, through work and creation, allow our true selves to emerge—are we able to become whole and to heal.

Without knowing that old tale, I had taken a similar course. The loss of Katherine had been the cutting off of my hands. After Katherine's deterioration, I carried the guilt of having been unable to protect my child, of failing to safeguard one of the most precious things in my life. How had I been so careless? On the outside, I looked fine. Emotionally, I was as maimed as the handless maiden.

Now I realize that, like the handless maiden, I literally went to the woods—we live in the mountains west of Denver—to heal. Each day when the children were at school, I wrote, and walked or ran to a ridge several miles from our house. I created a routine of aloneness that included long periods in the forest. My woods were literal as well as symbolic: I spent hours exploring the hillsides near my home and moved into the murky area of my unconscious, listening to my dreams, forcing myself to get up at night and jot them down before they evaporated.

There were times of extreme loneliness, and there were times when I experienced an unexpected sense of completeness. During those years, I crafted my journal entries into *Grief Dancers: A Journey into the Depths of the Soul*, the story of life with Katherine. I gave Katherine, who cannot speak, a voice.

I had always sought the miracle of a cure for Katherine. I wanted her to wake up one morning and start walking and talking. I wanted to be one of the lucky ones who beat the odds. By the time the book was finished, a different type of miracle had occurred: I'd stopped hurting. I never thought I'd get there. Before writing, I'd sidestepped my sorrow, not knowing how to move through it. The terrible ache, I believed, would always be there. Writing changed that. I got to a place where instead of leaving Katherine's room sad, I left her room filled with peace. Instead of dreading time with her, her smile filled me with happiness. Somewhere along the writing path, I let go of my dream for a normal Katherine and arrived at a place of acceptance and love.

This is a book about writing to heal the soul. It is a helping hand offered with the hope that you will complete your journey more quickly than I. It gives you exercises and examples to help you heal yourself, as only you can do. It has been created with the belief that you are about to set out on the most important life journey you will ever take.

There is now extensive research that shows writing—the simple act of putting down your deepest thoughts and feelings on paper—is one of the most powerful and effective means to ease and ultimately heal sorrow. The act of writing brings a structure and order to the chaos of grief. It taps into the healing power of your own unconscious. By giving voice to fears, anger, and despair, by letting go of old dreams and hopes, our self-healing powers come into play. The soul knows what it needs to heal. Through writing, it will lead you where you need to go.

There is no specific sequence you must follow to obtain these benefits. Write! Just write! Silence the inner critic that tells you you aren't a "good enough" writer, or that your words aren't worthy. You may take many detours and go off on side roads. The journey allows different routes to the destination. There are no wrong turns. Yet, the research also shows that there are several simple techniques you should use to reap the healing benefits of your writing:

- Write about your deepest thoughts and feelings.
- Write in a place where you will not be interrupted.
- Write frequently—daily, if possible—not less than three or four times a week.
- Write for yourself only, not for an audience.
- Seek professional help if you are wrestling with serious depression. Writing might well be one part of your broader therapy, but don't rely upon it alone.

Don't be surprised if you feel sad immediately after writing. This is difficult but life-enhancing work. Feeling the full impact of your loss is part of that process. Tears help us heal. Keep at it.

The benefits will come. There is no pat formula or one "right way" to do this kind of writing. It isn't like learning German or calculus. You already know, at the deepest level, how to heal yourself. You already have those resources. The point is to be honest, to write about what you really care about, and to shed your inhibitions on the page. You should not feel guilty if you write the "unspeakable." When we confront loss, we experience the full range of emotions—hatred, anger, disgust, disdain, despair, helplessness. That is okay. Don't feel guilty if you miss a day or a week or even a month of writing. Just always come back to it. Don't make it a burden. But keep at it. Writing allows you to access your wider mind, a wiser, more encompassing place deep within. Your story will unfold and through the writing of it, you will honor and embrace your sorrows, grow from them, and arrive at a place where life is more full and more joyful than you ever thought possible.

Where do I begin? How do I describe a process that is so personal, so intimate, so haphazard? How do I describe the need I had to sit in silence, open my notebook, and begin day after day, not knowing what might appear? How do I describe the initial trepidation, the times of quiet when no words came, the hours when words flowed like a rushing river that nothing could keep within its banks? How do I let people know that only through writing was I able to let go of my dreams for Katherine and love her as she is, and my life as it is? How do I describe the mysterious alchemy that transmutes our personal grief, anger, and incomprehension into a spaciousness of heart and mind?

CHAPTER I

Going Through Pain

Writing is a long process of introspection; it is a voyage toward the darkest

caverns of consciousness, a long, slow meditation. I write feeling my way in

silence, and along the way discover particles of truth, small crystals that fit in

the palm of one hand and justify my passage through this world.

—ISABEL ALLENDE, *Paula*

WE SKIED HIGHER THAN I'D EVER SKIED BEFORE, up the backbone of the Rockies to the top of Elk Mountain, my first winter ascent. Not a breath of wind stirred, though crisp waves of snow lay crusted around us, a testament to the wind's usual howling force. The blue of the sky blinded us. We had left our house in a storm the day before, sure that the skiing at Janet's Hut would be in a blizzard.

It was midafternoon when we set out to bag Elk Mountain, an easy climb of rhythmic traverses up the mountain's broad north flank to its 12,800-foot peak. At the summit, a 360-degree panorama unfolded, stretching from Capitol Peak near Aspen to the Mount Zirkel wilderness area near Steamboat Springs to the peaks of the Gore and Ten-Mile Ranges. Paul and I were flying high, proud of making it to the summit with more experienced mountaineers.

On the way down, we relaxed. Paul and I glided down a long ridge. Geoff and David, expert skiers, stopped higher on the crest, searching for a steep pitch for some good telemark turns. They dallied as Paul and I skied on to the lowest point on the ridge and a less precipitous descent. We had begun wide turns when we heard a sound I'd never heard before, a muffled roar reminiscent of an oncoming train. I saw a cloud of white a couple hundred feet away. The snow shifted so fast and effortlessly that it took me several seconds to realize it was an avalanche and several seconds more to realize that I didn't know where Geoff and David were. I skied toward Paul, looking down to where the snow had already piled deep at the base of the mountain. Then I saw Geoff skiing toward us and spotted David at the top of the slope, above the slide, safe and heading slowly down to where we waited.

"God, that was amazing!" Geoff said as he joined us.

"What happened?" I asked.

"I started down, then fell. Something told me I had to get up real fast."

I looked up to the bare mountainside and saw Geoff's tracks. He had skied across the path of the avalanche to safety. Had he stayed down another second, he would have been swept away.

We gathered at the bottom of the slope and looked up the hillside—now scarred with a one-hundred-foot-wide swath of exposed dirt—and down to where the snow lay like huge concrete slabs thrown together in a haphazard pile at an abandoned construction site. We jabbered about how unexpected it was, how fast it happened, the angle of the slope, the early winter–snow conditions. We all knew how close it had been, but we couldn't talk about how lucky we were to be standing there, instead of desperately shoveling, searching for buried friends.

After a while, my knees started shaking, and I couldn't feel my toes. I had to start moving to keep from freezing. I headed back to the hut, skiing as fast as I've ever skied, looking back every now and then at the marred hillside.

Crises hit like avalanches. Everything is going fine. Then all of a sudden, the earth shifts. It can be a cancer diagnosis, a car accident, the complications of childbirth, the death of a friend, the arrest of a child, the loss of a job, the end of a marriage. Dreams shatter, and we fear the pieces of our lives can never be glued together again. We cry out, but no one can hear us. We fall deeper into darkness and have no idea if we'll ever see light again.

Geoff is alive today because instinct told him he had to get up and ski on. He literally had to move through the avalanche. He couldn't turn back. He couldn't even hesitate. He had to keep going.

Sometimes we have no choice but to pick ourselves up and ski through the avalanches of our lives. We have to keep moving, or we'll be swept away. We can't stop and reflect, or we'll find ourselves buried under the weight of the tragedy.

Yet we need to understand that what is functional at one point may be dysfunctional at another. After the initial shock, we have to move from surviving to thriving. That can only be done when we acknowledge, and ultimately embrace, the full extent of the loss; when we go through our grief. If we don't, we die, or something in us dies.

But how do we go through grief? How do we set out on that path when we don't know what it looks like or where it begins? How do we start when we have no idea of the distance and no clue when we'll be done? We know what it means to "go through" school, or "go through" a car wash, or "go through" a maze, but what does it mean to go through grief?

I thought I was going through grief for many years. I thought I was doing exactly what I needed to do to "get on with it." In fact, getting on with it was part of my problem. I had not slowed down enough to allow myself to enter into the full scope and depth of the loss. My belief that I could "fix" Katherine ruled my life for the first five years. The next seven were spent in an upheaval of creation—three more children, a new organization—to avoid dealing with the loss of my first, deeply precious creation. During those years, I told myself, *Kat won't change me. Kat won't slow me down.* I could handle it all, or so I believed.

How naive I was to think that having a handicapped child who depended upon others for all of her needs wouldn't dramatically change my life. Kat's presence and the daily task of caring for her has permeated every fiber of my being. I wish I had admitted that sooner. I wish I had recognized and embraced the full magnitude of my loss. I realize now that part of going through grief involves entering fully into the tragedy, acknowledging the enormity of what has happened, and understanding that something profound has been taken away forever.

Isak Dinesen once said, "Any sorrow can be borne, if you can turn it into a story." With our writing, we honor the extent of our losses. We give details, we exaggerate, we express our pain, we share our greatest fears. Through writing, we discover unexpected particles of truth that light our path; we move through our grief mindfully, in a way that allows us to comprehend and integrate the experience into our lives, not just rush frantically on as the avalanche thunders around us. By going deep within to a place of honesty untainted by society's "shoulds," our vision is enlarged. We gain perspective on our lives.

Your Sacred Healing Journal

Start at the very beginning. You need a notebook, the simpler the better. A bright-colored spiral notebook—like the kind you had in school—is perfect, or one of those composition notebooks with the black-and-white marbled covers. Your notebook must not intimidate you. It can't be too elegant, because then you will feel that you can only write "finished" work in it. You'll be uncomfortable with scribbles and meanderings. You'll feel like you can't write sentimental junk (we all do) or that you can't rant and rave (we all do). You'll search too carefully for words, and in this notebook your words need to flow unchecked like a mountain stream. So make it cheap. Choose a size that feels comfortable to you. I use a 9 ½-by-6-inch size because it fits into my big leather purse, and I can carry it wherever I go and jot thoughts as they come.

Each exercise in this book is a starting place only. Don't feel constrained by it. The important thing is to write about your deepest thoughts and feelings. If an exercise spurs that, use it. If it doesn't, move on. If you find yourself going back to certain exercises, fine. Writing about the same thing repeatedly from slightly different angles is a healthy part of the process. You create new dimensions. You gain distance and clarity.

All of the exercises are designed so that you can write them in less than an hour, but it isn't necessary to carve out that much time. It works very well to do "short writes": Set aside fifteen to thirty minutes a day and "let 'er rip." The important thing is to keep writing and to write frequently. To give yourself the gift of a quiet place where you won't be interrupted. To avoid the excuses "I'm too tired today, too busy, too this, or too that." The slogan "Just do it" applies here. Go for it. Spill your guts.

You'll need to do some exercises numerous times as you explore different avenues. You'll finish others after one "write." You will discover what works best for you. One tip: Always write as quickly as your hand will allow. You are searching for first thoughts. Don't be concerned about spelling or grammar. Don't worry if you're not saying it exactly right. You can edit later if you wish. The point is to get your uncensored voice onto the page.

This writing is for you and you alone. It is for your heart and your health. It is *your* sacred healing journal. Use it only for this journey. It is not meant to be revealed.

At wedding receptions of members of my large extended family, we have the FHB rule. Whenever anyone whispers, "FHB," we know exactly what it means: "Family Hold Back" (such as on the shrimp!). In your journal, use the DHB rule: "Don't Hold Back." Don't be constrained. Down the road, you may want to burn your journal or share parts of it with someone you love, or possibly with the world. But right now, it is for you only. Think of it as a sculpture that you are creating with the most precious stones of your life.

Honor the Magnitude of Your Loss

You have a story—a very important story, a story that rests at the core of your being—to tell. It is a story that has torn your heart into pieces, and it is a story of beauty, because your heart couldn't have been torn without your having first loved and somehow lost something that you loved. Now is the time to begin honoring your story. A friend sent me a note that said simply, "Blessed are the cracked, for they shall let the light in." Remember that as you write.

Put all distractions aside—no phone, no children, no television. Light a candle or set a cup of tea by your side. Play soothing music. Create a safe and comforting place. Get in a comfortable position. To clear your head and calm your nerves, spend several minutes breathing deeply. You need to be centered to begin, and you need to breathe away your fears. You are going back to the beginning.

Exercise: The Turning Point

Some losses happen at a specific moment: the car accident, HIV diagnosis, stillbirth. Others occur over time: the unraveling of a marriage, chronic illness, bankruptcy. There is a point when you realize your life will be forever changed. When did you get the phone call, the diagnosis, the pink slip? When did the severity of the prognosis sink in? When did the inability to salvage the relationship become appallingly clear? Go back to that time and place. It seems impossibly difficult. But it is where we must start. Shakespeare said,

"Give sorrow words." That is what we are doing. Capture the scene. Where were you? How were you dressed? Who else was there? What did the place look like? How did you feel? What did you do? When did the fear set in? Did someone let you down? Who? How? Write down all the details. Let your hand, not your head, be your guide. Be specific. Don't strive for perfection. Be as negative, angry, frustrated, aggravated, whiny, ornery, disgusted, disdainful, despairing as you wish. DHB. Begin with "I remember. . . ." Keep your hand moving for fifteen minutes. Cry. It's okay. It's good. Tears release our pent-up emotions. They bring them to the surface of our lives and let them flow out. They are healing waters. Write through the tears.

You took the plunge. You have begun your sacred journal. You are brave. Celebrate your new adventure. And write again tomorrow.

CHAPTER 2

Expectations Revisited

Life is difficult. This is a great truth, one of the greatest truths. It is a great

truth because once we truly see this truth, we transcend it. Once we truly

know that life is difficult—once we truly understand and accept it—

then life is no longer difficult. Because once it is accepted, the fact that

life is difficult no longer matters.

—M. SCOTT PECK

As I LOOK AROUND, I SEE ONE FRIEND WHO HAS just ended a marriage of twenty-three years; another whose husband was recently convicted of sexual harassment; another who has diabetes that she can't control; another whose "perfect" adopted baby has muscular dystrophy; another whose sister died of breast cancer; another whose daughter is in prison on drug convictions; another who was fired two years ago and is still job-hunting; another whose son has Down syndrome; another who struggles with the scars of childhood sexual abuse; another whose brother is dying of AIDS; another whose father drank himself to death; another who at his prime was diagnosed with Parkinson's disease; another whose husband died in a plane crash, leaving her with two toddlers; another whose fiancé was killed in a car accident; another whose wife had to forgo a brilliant academic career because of epilepsy; another who is in a violent marriage and doesn't know how to get out; another whose thirteen-year-old granddaughter is pregnant. The list goes on. Let's face it, this isn't how we thought it would be.

In the movie *Beyond Rangoon*, U Aung Ko, a Burmese professor reduced to being a tour guide because his political activity prevents him from teaching, encounters a character played by Patricia Arquette, an American tourist mourning the violent deaths of her husband and son. He offers to show her some sights in Rangoon. During the day of touring, political tension mounts when the people demonstrate for human rights in the face of rifle-toting soldiers. Anticipating a military crackdown, the government orders all tourists to leave the country. As Arquette readies to depart, she discovers her passport has been stolen. She can't leave. She is swept into a revolutionary maelstrom, with U Aung Ko steering her through extraordinarily dangerous territory—both psychological and geographic. She must deal with her personal chaos and suffering against the backdrop of a country whose discord and sorrow mirror hers. During their attempt to escape to Thailand, U Aung Ko says to Arquette, "You must remember, suffering is the one promise life always keeps." By articulating that "promise," he both embraces and lets go of his sorrow in the same instant. He moves beyond the crazed reality of a country in upheaval to a place of wisdom and acceptance. He can face whatever the future holds.

There is an old Tibetan tale about a young woman, Krisha Gotami, who gave birth to a much-loved son. When her firstborn was a year old, he fell ill and died. Grief-stricken, Krisha Gotami walked through her city, holding the small body in her arms, begging for medicine to bring the child back to life. Some people ignored her; others laughed at her. Still others thought she was mad. Finally she came to a wise man who told her the only person on Earth who could help her was Buddha. She went to Buddha and recounted her tale. He listened carefully, then told Krisha Gotami he would help her if she would go into the city and bring him a mustard seed from the first home she came to that had not known death.

Elated, Krisha Gotami ran to the city and knocked on the door of the first house she encountered. "Buddha has sent me to retrieve a mustard seed from a house that has never known death," she said. "This is not a good house," said the owner. "We have known death here." She went to the next house and was told the same, and on to the next, and the next, until she had knocked on the door of every house in the city and remained unable to fulfill Buddha's request.

Having learned about the universality of suffering, she was able to bury her child, bid him farewell, and tell Buddha, "I understand what you were trying to teach me. I was too blinded by my own grief to see that we all suffer."

This is a hard lesson, particularly in a country graced with prosperity, stability, and the "can do," problem-solving American outlook. Our expectations of life are high. We tend to view health, wealth, and happiness as a "promise" life makes to us. The shock is severe when, inevitably, that promise is not kept. Moreover, the unrealistic expectations can blind us to the richness a less-than-perfect life holds.

Frank McCourt, the author of *Angela's Ashes* and a New York City teacher for thirty years, taught me this in a session with Denver teachers. What I most remember was a question one teacher asked him. "We talk a lot about resilience," she began. "You lived in a slum, nearly starved to death, had an alcoholic father, and a ninth-grade education in crummy schools. How did you make it?"

"I didn't see it that way," McCourt said, lowering his voice. "My childhood was very rich. There was this gang of us. We were on the streets all the time playing and laughing. We had no TV, no radio. But we had each other, and we never wanted to go home when our mothers started calling us in for dinner. I suppose because we had nothing, we appreciated everything."

He went on to tell about the one woman in his neighborhood who had a radio. It had been given by the government to her crippled mother who lived with her. The neighbors were all jealous. "Each night I prayed for a crippled grandma," McCourt chuckled. On Sunday evenings, the woman placed the radio on the windowsill and turned it up loud. That was the night the BBC broadcast a Shakespeare play. The kids clustered beneath the window, listening. "Those voices, that language. It was magic. The highlight of my week." In the midst of grinding poverty, McCourt developed a love of stories and gift of language that sustained and enriched him, his students, and eventually millions of readers. Of course, indigence is not bliss, and *Angela's Ashes* also shows the dehumanizing aspect of poverty. But how McCourt survived and eventually triumphed holds an important lesson. He expected no more than he had. With a child's guilelessness, he embraced both the sorrow and the laughter around him, and his life was rich.

As children, many of us fell asleep to the happily-ever-after of fairy tales and played dress-ups in which we created our own stories of princes and princesses. With the help of parents, friends, and society, we created expectations of what our lives would be.

Inescapably, somewhere along the way our expectations were shattered. The good health, the happy marriage, the healthy children, the dream job, the perfect house didn't materialize in the way we planned; or worse, we had it but lost it.

Perhaps we would do our children a service if we changed the typical fairy-tale ending to "and they lived happily after great suffering." Perhaps that is the message that U Aung Ko, Krisha Gotami, and Frank McCourt share. If our expectations included loss, we would handle our lives better and fear our losses less. Perhaps we would come to understand that when we move through our losses, they wrench open our hearts and expand our minds.

While we would be fools to seek out sorrow, the unavoidable suffering that is an integral part of life's fabric is not something to view as a cross that we bear alone. It simply is. And, as such, it is one of life's great teachers, presenting us with opportunities to expand our souls and deepen our understanding and compassion.

Articulate Your Expectations

A large part of coming to terms with loss is dealing with our expectations of what "should have been." Until we articulate those expectations, we cannot move beyond them. We are stuck in the "Why me?" litany. We feel singled out and wonder what we did to deserve such a nightmare. We review our lives and speculate that we are being punished for that time we shoplifted or lied to our parents or had a love affair or cheated on an exam or prayed the opposing quarterback would break his leg or failed to visit Great-aunt Ellie in the nursing home. We think of all the missteps we've taken. We vaguely remember Jonathan Edward's "Sinners in the Hands of an Angry God" sermon from high school and fear there might be truth in his grim Puritan message. We are miserable, at some level convinced we brought our misfortunes upon ourselves. Fear of the future paralyzes us with anxiety. How will we cope? How will we make it through this disaster?

At the same time, we have a vision of what our lives were supposed to be. This, definitely, is *not* it. We have experienced a series of little deaths as our expectations crumbled. It is essential that we mourn the loss of those expectations, which shaped our mind-sets and created our personal worldviews.

Exercise: How It Was Supposed to Be

Set out in detail what you were going to do. Go back as far as you can. Go to when you were a child and started to imagine your life.

Think back to how you were "told" it would be, what you told yourself it would be. Write about those expectations. Begin this exercise with "I was going to. . . ."

Exercise: What Did You Expect?

Now, zero in on the expectations you created around a specific relationship, love, friendship, or your family, career, children. Choose one thing. What had you expected it to be? What did that mean in your life? Write for fifteen minutes, nonstop.

Exercise: A Change of Plans

The third part of this exercise begins with "But I didn't plan. . . ." (I didn't plan to get divorced. I didn't plan not to marry. I didn't plan to be childless. I didn't plan to have cancer. I didn't plan to take care of my mother. I didn't plan to have to work all my life. I didn't plan to watch my child die. I didn't plan to get multiple sclerosis. I didn't plan to have a car accident. I didn't plan to drop out of school to have a baby.) Take several deep, centering breaths. Now write for at least fifteen minutes.

CHAPTER 3

Trying to Fix It

Writing is the most profound way of codifying your thoughts, the best way of

learning from yourself who you are and what you believe.

—Warren Bennis, *On Becoming a Leader*

On a damp August day twenty years ago, I walked on an overgrown coastal path north of Seattle. Paul followed a few steps behind. Fog rolled in as steamers cruised the gray waters of Puget Sound. An ocean breeze blew. The smell of salt water permeated the air. Ferns brushed my legs, creating a dank cold film on my skin. I felt more at one with that lush country than I'd ever thought possible. Like it, I was—for the first time—a creator. I tilted my back and cupped my hands beneath my huge stomach.

We hiked a couple of miles, wrapped in our thoughts, holding hands, then letting go where the path narrowed, hardly speaking. The blast of fog whistles brought a paradoxical thought. I ached to hold the baby in my arms, and I was afraid: I feared I wouldn't have what it takes to raise a child. The phrase "three's a crowd" played through my mind. But I didn't really have a clue.

Back in the car, my first words were "I'm starved." The brisk air and walking had done their work.

We drove toward the Pike Street Market. "I have this funny feeling I'm looking for something real specific, but I don't know what it is," I told Paul.

Minutes later, we rounded a corner. Down the street hung a dark green sign with "Raison d'Être" inscribed in gold. "That's it," I said as I pointed. "Look—'A Reason for Being.' Can you believe it?"

We walked into rich smells of brewing coffee and heating croissants, brocade upholstery and forest-green walls, the Sunday *New York Times*, and classical music. Once the bowls of raspberries and plates of chocolate croissants were set before us, I was sure that the perfection of Raison d'Être was a good omen for the life to come.

A month later, Katherine was born. For her first year, she was—like that café in Seattle—perfect. From her, I learned to love in a way I'd never loved before. Yet I was young and not really prepared for what loving Katherine would mean.

Around the time Katherine was a year old, the changes began. Subtly, but suddenly. Over the course of a few months, her smiles were replaced by grimaces, her chortles by low moans or silence. She started grinding her teeth, wringing her hands all day, and screaming at night. Her eyes crossed. She lost interest in toys. Hospital and doctor visits consumed our lives, but the diagnostic tests told us nothing. Katherine slipped further away.

During that time, I would put Kat in her crib, go to my bedroom, sit on the floor, and weep. Sometimes I'd force myself to close my eyes and return to Raison d'Être. I'd escape the reality I couldn't accept and fly away to that mental refuge, a place of calm that held my lost innocence. It had become my personal "calm before the storm" image, unshakably lodged in my brain. And I would wonder what my reason for being was if I couldn't even protect my child from the mysterious illness that was attacking her.

Months passed. I undertook a crazed effort to cure Kat, to do whatever was necessary to retrieve the laughter and responsiveness of her first year. I had a new raison d'être. If I was good and worked hard, I would be rewarded. That's what I'd always been taught. If I just set my mind to it, I could "fix" her. I was sure of it. We began endless trips to doctors, specialists, hospitals. We tried speech, occupational, and physical therapies, special preschools, faith healers, holy dirt, macrobiotic diets, and finally patterning—an intensive-therapy program that involved one hundred volunteers coming to our house each week. But after three years of patterning, Katherine was five years old, still wore diapers, and couldn't walk, talk, or feed herself. By then, my hope for a normal life for her had faded.

And I came to realize that the hardest part of the journey wasn't cooking the special foods or rushing from one therapy program to the next or working fourteen hours a day to retrain Katherine's brain. It was letting go of my hope for a normal life for her, because that meant I had to learn to accept her as she was—handicapped, wordless, totally dependent.

When Katherine was seven, and finally diagnosed with Rett syndrome, a neurological disease with no known cause or cure, we learned that nothing we did or could have done would have altered the course of her life. Her fate was set at the moment of conception.

Slow learner that I am, I've come to realize—after much time, grief, denial, and sadness—that Katherine was put here for a noble purpose. Her raison d'être has been to teach us about unconditional love, and the strength and grace that come from accepting others exactly as they are—no matter how hurt, no matter how different. She taught me that I couldn't make her well, but I could reach deep within myself and open my heart so that I could embrace her crippled body and love her spirit. She taught me that my raison d'être wasn't to fix her, but through her to know myself better so that I might fix the only person I ever had the power to fix—myself.

Acknowledging What We Can Do and What We Can't

We live in a fix-it culture. We want quick solutions to complex problems—Motrin for a backache, Prozac for a bad day. But what happens when we confront something we can't fix? What happens when something that we don't choose, chooses us? I tried for years to fix Kat. I was bound and determined to retrieve my perfect baby. It literally took the soul-searching process of writing *Grief Dancers* for me to realize that I could never fix Kat and, what's more, that was okay.

We want to make things right, to take care of those dear to us, to keep them from harm. But we can do only what we can do. Beyond that, we have to trust in some greater power. We have to move beyond our hopes and dreams to a place of acceptance. And we have to realize that true, gut-level acceptance is an act of courage.

In *Man's Search for Meaning,* Viktor Frankl writes, "We who lived in concentration camps can remember the men who walked through the huts comforting others, giving away their last piece of bread. They may have been few in number, but they offer sufficient proof that everything can be taken from a man but one thing: the last of the human freedoms—to choose one's attitude in any given set of circumstances, to choose one's way."

In other words, even imprisoned in the most evil place imaginable, living in monstrous and brutal conditions, with all freedoms removed, we nonetheless retain the ultimate freedom: the power to choose our response to our circumstances. No one can take away that power, no matter how extreme the pain and loss. We can choose to be broken by the loss of a child, or we can celebrate that child's time on this earth. We can choose to be bitter about a cancer diagnosis, or we can choose to learn everything we can about life from the experience. We can bemoan the loss of a job, or we can view it as an opportunity to try something new. It is not that life is without tragedies. It is that tragedies are a part of life, and life goes on regardless of how we choose to respond to our personal losses.

Exercise: The Unfixable

Is there something in your life that you can't fix? Write about it. Write about all the things you did to try to fix it. Write about how you felt about not being able to fix it. Did you get angry, bitter, numb? There aren't "right" ways to respond to a life loss, but you do need to be honest and look deeply at how you chose—and are today choosing—to react to the circumstances thrown your way. Begin with "I tried everything in my power. . . ."

Exercise: What You Can and Cannot Control

Change gears. Now write about what is/was in your control and what is/was not. (I can look for a new job, get excellent medical care, go to family counseling, create a support system; I cannot cure my husband's cancer, force my lover to get therapy, fix my child's brain, stop my company from downsizing.) Begin with "I can. . . ." List everything you can do. Then shift to "I cannot. . . ." List everything that you cannot do.

CHAPTER 4

Learning from Others

Courage is a greater virtue than love. At best, it takes courage to love.

—Paul Tillich

L ENA HAD DYED BLACK HAIR, CHIPPED RED NAILS, dark circles under her eyes, a mouth that turned down at the edges, tight black slacks, and a pink polyester shirt stretched taut across her chest. An emergency-room nurse, she worked the night shift at Denver General, usually handling victims of stabbings, rapes, and car accidents. "You can't believe the people I deal with." Her dry laugh bared yellow teeth. She took a deep drag on a cigarette and added that her three-year-old adopted daughter had AIDS.

Judy was a slender, dark-haired woman with an open face and upbeat attitude. She wore blue jeans, a blue-jean vest, lace shirt, and large-heeled, black boots. Her four-year-old son had leukemia.

Elise's ten-year-old son couldn't grow skin. His body was covered with bandages to keep it literally from falling apart. Through thick smudged mascara, she looked tired, beaten down by sadness. "I'm not sure how to deal with these years," she said. "Lauren was seven when Drew was born. Now she's seventeen—grown up—and I didn't even notice until it was too late."

We were four mothers who had come together in a small seminar to create our "sacred bodies," to take a journey inward beyond our hurt children and busy lives to a place where we better understood what we held sacrosanct.

After introductions, Gina, the instructor, took a rawhide drum from the wall and began to thump it lightly. "Relax, breathe slowly. Leave your worries behind." Gina spoke in a low, rhythmic voice. "Now in your minds, I want you to go to the mountains or the sea. Close your eyes and imagine waves rushing against the shore or snow-topped peaks or a grassy meadow. Smell the spray of the sea or the scent of pine." We rested in the womblike peace of the darkened room as Gina spoke and our thoughts meandered.

When the lights were turned on, Gina handed me a carved talking stick decorated with beads and leather. Following the Native-American tradition, we passed the stick among us, speaking only when we held the stick, holding it like a friend's hand as we spoke about the places we had traveled during the guided meditation.

When Lena's turn came, she said, "I went to the mountains for a while, then I came right back here. I couldn't seem to get away. Sorry." She passed the stick quickly to Judy.

When we finished sharing, dozens of magazines, plastic cartons full of glitter, sequins, bric-a-brac, buttons, and glue sticks were brought out. We began to create our sacred bodies. First we helped each other trace the outline of our bodies on poster board, choosing whatever shape we wanted. I curved on my side, assuming my sleeping position, not realizing until after the outline had been drawn that mine was a loose fetal curl. Lena lay down with her arms outstretched and her legs crossed. When she had cut out her silhouette, I saw that it would have fit perfectly on a crucifix. Judy and Elise both lay on their backs with their legs spread and their arms at their sides. We cut out our shapes and began flipping through magazines, clipping pictures that reminded us of something in our lives, selecting decorations that struck our fancy, laughing at the absurdity of grown women playing preschool games, a bit nervous about how our sacred bodies would evolve.

I particularly wondered what Lena would make of hers, but I never found out. She only came to that one session, though there were three more as part of the course. I guess at some level she didn't really belong. Life had been too concrete for her to spend time creating a fantasy journey. She'd had plenty of real ones. As we worked, I asked her about her daughter, Natalie, who was then three. "How did you choose her?" I asked.

"I didn't choose her," she coughed. "It was real obvious who did the choosing. She chose me."

"How do you mean?"

"When I first saw her, I turned away. I couldn't look," she said. "And trust me, I've seen everything. It was an emergency C-section. The mom hadn't been to a doctor once during the pregnancy. The baby was too small and too fragile. She was on a one-way course to death. Her mom was an addict, didn't know who the father was. I had this urge to wring the mother's neck.

"I was in the operating room, and it was chaos. All the attention was on the mother at first, and then we shifted to the baby. I've never seen anything so helpless. We were wheeling her into the neonatal unit when our eyes locked. I can't describe it. I realized in that second that the buck stopped with me, that there was no one else. My husband had walked out years ago. I'd raised two kids. The last thing I needed was a baby. But I didn't have a choice. That baby had chosen me. There was no doubt about it. I was the chosen one, not her. All I could do was take her home and love her. The adoption went quickly. No one else wanted her."

As Lena spoke, I wondered about the power of the innocent; how that tiny infant could have reached out and found a savior at that critical juncture in her life; how a newborn, with grim life prospects, could open a heart so quickly. I marveled at Lena's willingness to take on the burden of caring for a dying child who would bring her great heartache and loss, because the more she loved her, the more she would have to lose.

"It hasn't been easy," Lena said, looking toward the window, "but it was the right thing to do. No regrets."

There are heroes all around us and we don't know it. They wouldn't think of themselves that way; yet there they are. They've walked right through their fear. They've discovered their courage. And they've quietly done the right thing, asking for nothing in return.

"How lucky she is," I remarked.

"No. You've got it backward," Lena said. "I'm the lucky one."

Heroes Who Teach Us

When we start writing our stories, we begin to discover aspects of our lives that we didn't know existed. Through this process of unearthing, of digging beneath the surface layer to something richer and darker, we find the gems within. And, as we talk about what we write, we become more aware of other people's gems. People we might dismiss without a thought reveal themselves to us, often in stunning ways. They become three-dimensional as we listen. And they become inspirations: If they can do it, so can we. Sharing stories gives us perspective. We begin to understand that while our road has been rugged, we are not alone. We find people who have struggled more, who have taken on even greater challenges. We're inspired by the way they've chosen to chart their difficult courses. We see their strength and humanity, and it helps us find our own.

Step out of yourself for a moment. Think about a conversation you've had that was full of surprises, where you learned something about someone that you never would have expected. I have a poet friend, Sophia, whose father committed suicide after the Korean War, leaving behind four children; whose brother later committed suicide; whose sister died of AIDS. Sophia, a single mom, has adopted her sister's son and is raising him with her own children. And Sophia, who is nearly fifty, glows with the beauty of having loved and survived. Another friend, an outdoor buddy in her mid-thirties with two young children, almost died of breast cancer two years ago. After the chemotherapy, as a way to heal, she took up triathalons. Renata, a woman whose teenage Sioux mother abandoned her and whose African-American father was unable to raise her, was shuffled from relative to relative as a child and ended up in an Indian boarding school. Renata went on to be a teacher, obtained her law degree, and today is a brilliant mentor, helping people of color realize their dreams and preserving Native-American stories. Debra lived through a tough childhood with an alcoholic father and then two abusive marriages. She raised six children, working one odd job after another. She chose to deal with the struggles of her past by caring for others. She has "adopted" two elderly women. She visits them weekly in their nursing homes, takes them to doctors' appointments, and includes them in holiday gatherings.

These stories are all around us: people whose courage gives us courage. Somehow they have broken through their pain and heartache and arrived at a place of strength and beauty. They are not weaker because of their travails, but stronger. They have experienced the dark night of the soul, struggled through it, and emerged in full sunlight. They are stronger in the broken places. They have not ignored or rejected their losses, but they have grown through them and from them. They have chosen to be better, not bitter. Their fortitude and sheer pluck give us a different view of how to approach our own lives. You may not be ready to share your story with anyone else yet, but you're ready to listen to those of others, which can help the healing process.

Exercise: My Hero

Write about someone you know who has overcome adversity and who has been an inspiration to you. Think about how he or she has done it. Think about the unique aspects of his or her character that you admire because of the course he or she chose to take. This person inspires you because of the way he or she confronted a challenge. There are models out there who are our guides. You respect them more, not less, because of the difficulties they've encountered and the way they've chosen to cope and grow from their experiences. They give us energy and provide sustenance. We need them, like we need nurturing food and nature's beauty. Through their examples, they make it possible for us to chart more courageous and life-enhancing paths.

You can write about someone you know well or someone you sat next to in an airplane, spoke with for the entire trip, and never saw again; someone you read about in the newspaper or someone a friend told you about. When you write, imagine the full range of feelings that he or she experienced. Imagine that person's sorrows and triumphs. Get inside his or her skin. Write about what you would have feared the most in that situation and how you see that person today because of his or her choices. Begin with "_____ gives me courage because. . . ."

CHAPTER 5

Experiencing Death

Death is a vast mystery, but there are two things we can say about it:

It is absolutely certain that we will die, and it is uncertain when

or how we will die.

— SOGYAL RINPOCHE, *The Tibetan Book of Living and Dying*

M Y OWN FIRST EXPERIENCE OF DEATH OCCURRED when I was eleven, living in a small town in Ohio. Woodsfield was the county seat, a rural community with a Main Street that had a five-and-dime with a soda fountain, a theater that charged twenty-five cents for a movie ticket, a dress shop, a three-story hotel, a restaurant, and a grocery store where the owner stood behind his counter and reached for the items you pointed out, which were neatly stacked on the shelves behind him.

It was before the Vietnam War, before drugs and alcohol were issues for teens. Chewing gum in class and wearing short skirts were serious offenses. Every now and then, a teacher would have a girl in class kneel beside her desk. If her skirt touched the ground, she passed. If not, she was sent home and asked to come back in something "more decent."

There were no sports for girls, and it was made clear early on that the girls' job was to cheer the boys to victory. Most of us did it without thinking, questioning, or wondering why physical competition was exclusively a male prerogative.

I can't even remember his name now. Frank, I think. The older brother of the head cheerleader, a wild guy with a James Dean haircut and swagger to match. "Too handsome for his own good," the gossips would chatter. "That boy's out of control!" I somehow knew they were right.

Up the street from our house was the local hangout, Berry's. Booths hugged the back wall; a wooden counter stretched to the left of the entrance; red vinyl stools bolted to the floor lined the counter. I'd spin until I was dizzy and was never told to knock it off. Mainly high-school kids hung out there. But every now and then, my friend Linda and I slipped in for a bowl of chili and a grape soda. When Frank was there, I'd sit so I could look at him without his noticing me. I'd just watch him—the way he drank his Coke (always from a bottle), slowly with his head tilted back and his Adam's apple bouncing. He brushed his bangs back, but there was a lock of hair that curled and fell down over his forehead. He was slender with muscular forearms. He worked in a garage on weekends, and a couple of times I noticed grease stains on his clothes. When he was around, everything revolved around him. He was king, holding court.

Once I was in the checkout line when he queued up behind me. I could smell him, that combination of grease and sweat and Brylcreem, or whatever boys used back then to slick back their hair. My heart stopped. I turned my head. His eyes caught mine. He reached out, brushed his hand across the top of my head, and said, "How's it going, sport?" I couldn't speak. I just nodded, paid for a couple of bubble gums, and ran all the way home.

One morning, my parents were sitting at the kitchen table when I came down. "Look at this," my mother said, her coffee cup resting on the open paper. "How sad." The windows were open, and there was the smell of rotting leaves. "Frank Robinson got killed last night. Drag-racing down Main Street. Can you believe it? His car wrapped around a lamppost, they say. Died instantly."

All the kids at school talked about it that day, but I couldn't. Several days later, I heard there was going to be a viewing at the funeral home. I didn't know what that meant, but I knew I needed to go. I didn't tell my parents. Everything was within walking distance in Woodsfield. I took the shortcut across the school playground, up the alley, and on to the funeral parlor in an old Victorian house that I'd walked by hundreds of times but had never had the urge or need to enter. I had to get close to him one last time. It was a cool fall evening; I didn't have a coat.

Wood paneling darkened the entrance hall. People milled around. His mother stood crying in a corner and looked abnormally small and frail. I didn't see his sister. The carpet was murky and patterned. Frank lay in an open casket, as handsome as ever, but his skin was waxy and gray and there was none of the energy and none of his smell. I started to shiver and couldn't stop. I signed some guest book on the way out—my first name only—and ran all the way home. My heart beat so hard, I thought it would jump out of my body. I couldn't contain it. It hurt too much. Call it loss of innocence or coming of age, I knew I'd never totally lose that ache.

Contemplating Death

In our day-to-day lives, we often forget how fragile life is. We forget that death is a certainty and that for each of us it is only a matter of time. That reality was brought home at nearby Columbine High School where twelve students and a teacher were viciously killed and others seriously wounded by a couple of demented classmates who went on a murderous rampage. My children's school is on the same street, several miles north of Columbine. I was driving when I heard on the radio that a high school on South Pierce was under siege. My heart froze. Afterwards, when I realized my children were safe, I also realized how close they'd come to death and how terribly vulnerable we all are. In the aftermath of the Columbine atrocity, a student who had been in the school was interviewed on television. "You have to live life. That's what this has taught me," she said. "Things can change so fast. Just look. . . ." And then she started to cry.

When Frank died more than thirty years ago, I didn't know what to make of it. I was shaken and knew something precious had been snuffed out, but I couldn't enter into the full scope of the loss. I didn't have the words to articulate what I felt, and I didn't have the perspective to understand that death can be a wake-up call about how we live our lives. Frank's death, while vivid, taught me little. I forgot about it for decades. Only much later, after Katherine and the deaths of friends and relatives, did the import of Frank's short life cascade upon me.

There is power in contemplating death. By doing so, we think more about how we should live our lives. We focus more on what is important to us right now. We are forced to live more in the present, reminded of the preciousness of each moment. We open our hearts as we realize that we all are literally in the same boat, headed in the same direction. Thinking about death helps clear away the cobwebs of complacency and entitlement. It moves us closer to compassion for others and for ourselves.

Exercise: Facing Death

Write about death. Focusing on death is not a macabre exercise, but a tool for enhancing your life right now. Think about the exercises listed below, and choose one to do today. Come back to this list from time to time until you've done them all.

- Imagine your own death and write about how you lived up until that moment. Are you comfortable with the choices you made?

Would you live differently if you had known death was around the corner?

- Write about how you would live—exactly what you would do (or stop doing)—if you were told you have only six months to live.
- Think about the death of someone you loved. Write about how that person approached death and what that death has meant in your life. Write about the lessons you learned, the loss you feel, and the thoughts you continue to carry about that person.
- Write about your own first experience of death, the awakening to the fact of death's reality. This can be the death of a relative, a friend, an acquaintance, a public figure, or a beloved pet.

CHAPTER 6

Taking Things for Granted

Surrounded by my memories that night,

I took my pen and I began to write.

—Kuki Gallmann, *I Dreamed of Africa*

"ALOPECIA AREATA. WHAT A BEAUTIFUL SOUND," MY daughter Helen says as she brushes her hair and looks in the large bathroom mirror. "It's like an ancient rune in Tolkien." She lifts the hair on the right side of her head and looks carefully at the bald spots beneath. She pulls a large ball of hair from the brush and tosses it in the trash can.

I find tight wads of hair on towels, in corners, in the dryer. Slowly, daily, her hair falls out.

"Mom, when I had the strep test, the nurse looked at my hair and asked about chemotherapy. What did she mean?"

I explain about cancer. "Oh, Mom, I hoped it didn't show that much."

"The nurse's job is to look at you carefully. No one else can tell. Don't worry, you look great."

She pulls bows and barrettes from the drawer, trying to find a way to decorate her hair. Every style shows the bald spots. Finally, I bring out a handful of colorful bandanas. We wrap them around her head conjuring Africa, Egypt, Polynesia. A smile lights her face. The next day, we go to a children's store. In the dressing room, Helen tries on every cloth hair band in the shop.

Several years ago, I noticed a bald spot at the back of Helen's head. The bald spot grew until it stretched two inches across her scalp. We pulled her hair back and clasped it at the nape of her neck. Only when she swam did the bald circle show. We also began taking her to a psychologist, fearing the loss of her hair might be related to grief over Katherine. Little by little, it grew back.

This time, the hair is falling out all over her head. We cut bangs to hide the receding hairline, wisps of hair because so little is left. We curl and crimp the ends to create a fluffier look. At night we apply three ointments. Each morning, after she has washed the grease out of her hair, her brush is thick with hair, and more bald spots have appeared. I try to stay upbeat, to assure her how pretty she is, and act as if it doesn't matter. But without hair, it's as if she has no buffer from a sometimes hostile world.

I pick Helen up from school the first day after Christmas break. She runs to the car, holding down her hair with both hands as the wind blows it back, unveiling the bald spots. Her heavy backpack is slung over one shoulder and bounces awkwardly from chest to back. She gets into the car with tears in her eyes.

"Mom, when I was in the lunch line, this fourth-grade boy lifted up my hair and said, 'Hey, do you shave your head?' What could I say, Mom? There was nothing I could say. He'd never understand. I'm afraid other kids will start making fun of me. Sometimes, I just want to hide."

Alopecia areata. Unexplained hair loss. The doctors can't stop it, and it could be permanent.

She doesn't stand as straight. Her shoulders droop. She bows her head and avoids looking people in the eye. No longer does she have that surefooted stride. I start bringing her home for lunch—no more lunch lines with sharp-tongued boys who don't understand.

Wind shakes the house. I can't sleep. Wooden porch furniture slides from one side of the deck to the other. I am tired of those things in life that toss us back and forth with no guardrails to catch us. I can't wipe the picture of Helen's naked head from my mind. I can't forget the words hurled from unsuspecting class-mates that rip into her heart. Every day, with painstaking care, I look at her scalp with the hope of finding new hair growth, and wonder if I've made her feel better or worse with my own worry, which I hide behind good humor and feigned confidence in her recovery.

"Let's call it a hairpiece. *Wig* is too blunt," Helen says as she runs her fingers through the auburn waves.

That morning I had called wig shops all over Denver. I found Lila's name in the yellow pages. When I talked with her on the phone, I broke down. She agreed to come up to our house later that day to fit Helen for a wig. She had said, "I can't work miracles, but I come pretty close."

After school, Helen kept asking what time it was and when Lila was going to be there. Lila was an hour late when we got her call. She was lost on the dirt roads near our house. I drove out, found her, and led her back.

A small Asian woman with a lively, open face, Lila's thick black hair fell to her shoulders. She wore an oversize Hawaiian-print shirt, black stirrup pants, and black slip-on shoes. She lifted wig samples out of a canvas bag and spoke to Helen with concern, but never lost her directness. "Helen, you'll need to be strong. Think of all the good things. You're pretty, smart, healthy. . . ."

We spent an hour looking at hair-color samples and pictures of different wig styles. Then, Lila reached her hand to her head.

"Helen, could you tell I wear a wig?" She pulled off her wig, exposing her bald head.

Helen stared at Lila.

"I had no idea," I said.

"I want a wig just like that," Helen said.

"I have cancer. The chemo made me lose all my hair. Now, depending on what I feel like, I wear this wig or a real short one."

By the time Lila left, we had bought a shoulder-length synthetic-hair wig and ordered a real-hair wig that would arrive in six weeks.

That night, all Helen talked about was Lila and how pretty and brave she was. "If she can do it, so can I."

"The best day of my life," Helen wrote on her calendar in large letters with arrows pointing to the date February 3.

That day she sat on a wooden stool at the front of her fifth-grade class. "You may have noticed I'm losing my hair. I have a hair-loss disease. Most of my hair has fallen out. There's nothing I can do about it. That's why I'm wearing this wig." She scanned the class.

The children watched intently.

"It's been a really hard time for me. But I know it'll be all right. I want to tell you about the lady who got the wig for me. Her name is Lila. She helped me a lot. She has cancer. Because of the chemotherapy, she's lost all her hair and has to wear a wig. She has one long one and one short one. She stands tall and walks with pride. She doesn't let it slow her down. She's beautiful."

Helen asked if anyone had questions.

"Do you have cancer?"

"No. I'm healthy except for my hair."

"Will your hair grow back?"

"We think so, but I don't know for sure."

A cute, blond boy stood up, "Hey, Helen. I think you look better with the wig."

Every student joined him in standing, and clapped as Helen walked back to her seat.

Though it has not been easy growing up bald in a culture preoccupied with physical appearance, Helen has had many "best days" since that disclosure in her fifth-grade classroom. And her hair has not returned—no brows, no lashes. She is revealed. Through her revelation, she writes about the life around her, capturing the details of loss, sorrow, joy, and living in verse. She writes to make sense of Katherine's illness, my dark moods, her sister Alice's spicy personality, and her own baldness. She writes like a waterfall, never in drought. With the voice of a child, she has written through her pain and has turned it into art.

Unchangeable

When there are things I cannot change
—the passing of time, the darkness of heart—

I turn to other things I cannot change
—the color of the setting sky, the rugged outline of the
mountains—

There is something to knowing
—knowing if I weep the white stars will stay in pattern—

Secrets

There are secrets
Murmuring like growing things
Coming into my body
Whispering around inside like wind in the crags

Parched buffalo bones appear from the night
And make a song to the moon
Old chief of the Crow tells the sun to rise
Beckoning, a green sapling offered to dawn

The marks of the weathers
Or small human scratchings
Make wrinkles
In the permanence of canyon rock

There is a wide indian sky
A girl in the red earth
With a revealed head
She asks for some secrets

And begins to cover
Her nakedness
Paints
A clay pot

The Power of Appreciation

There is a close connection between our expectations and those things we take for granted. We expect certain people whom we value always to be there for us. Many places or things that we cherish, we expect to remain unchanged. Too often, those people or things that we care most about, we take for granted. We go through life in a daze of activity, rarely stopping in awe and wonderment, rarely slowing down long enough to take stock of the gifts that surround us. We understand too late what we had and then lost. *Now* is the time to appreciate what is dear to us—those people and things that are so integral to our lives that we fail to savor them.

Exercise: Appreciation

Start at the beginning of your day and list those people and things that add fundamental texture and meaning to your life. Be very specific about them. Here is one of my lists:

- waking next to Paul
- seeing the morning light through the blinds
- my first cup of coffee
- a walk at dawn
- a morning smile from my son, Mark
- Alice's pancakes

List thirty things that enhance your life that you don't usually think about and that could change. Write them quickly, happily. Include the big things and the little things. This is not a test. This is a listing, a quick write, a listening to your gut. List what comes to the surface of your mind.

Exercise: Loss

We have all lost something we cared about: a favorite childhood toy, a pet, a job, a grandparent, a friend, a lover, a house. It can be something little or something big. It has to be something that you missed terribly when it was gone. Think about what that person or thing meant to you. Why was it so important? Why had you cared so much about it? Why did its loss come as such a surprise? What dreams did its loss forever change? When did you appreciate it the most: while you still had it or after it was gone? Begin with "Once upon a time, I had. . . ."

CHAPTER 7

The Importance of Memory

The only life we know well, the one on which we are the ultimate authority,

is our own. The only experience to which we can bear witness is that which

we have personally endured or observed.

—WALLACE E. STEGNER, *Where the Bluebird Sings to the Lemonade Springs*

IT REMAINS A DUSKY, FOREBODING PLACE WHERE children speak in whispers and fat Pekingese dogs lumber up steep wood steps. The yellow Victorian house, my grandfather Nemo's family home, presented a stodgy, prim face to the world. Its wrought-iron fence opened at an intricate gate with a stubbornly rusted latch. A large porch stretched halfway around the first floor. A circular turret crowned its southwest corner. Thick velvet curtains hung at the windows. In the entrance hall, a huge coat stand with outstretched arms provided a stiff greeting. An oak staircase circled behind it.

On the north side of the house, the front parlor, middle parlor, and dining room were strung together like beads. I spent almost no time there. My days were spent with Biggie, Nemo's oldest sister, the firstborn of the eight Coleman children. By the time I knew Biggie, she was a short, fat lady with soft hands and white hair tightly pinned in a bun. On rare occasions, she let her hair down, and it tumbled like silk to her waist.

Biggie's pictures showed a lively, trim girl with an upturned nose and hair piled on her head. A young soldier courted her, the only man to whom she gave her heart: Billy died of tuberculosis when Biggie was in her early twenties. Her engagement ring passed down to my mother and on to my brother's wife. Ever since I could remember, Billy's picture sat in a plain silver frame on the mantel in Biggie's bedroom.

I imagine the yellow house eighty years ago when children scampered through its formal rooms to the gardens and beehives out back. Four of the Coleman children remained in their childhood home until their deaths, loners who never married and whose major outing was to walk across the street to the corner grocery. They became bizarre, loveable old people whose domineering mother had made it impossible for them to take flight. Even Nemo, a father of four daughters, stopped for a second breakfast with his mother every day.

Uncle Arboo—a dry old man addicted to Coca-Cola and Tums, who dated the same woman for thirty years—stood behind doorways in dark halls and jumped out at us, yelling, "Aw Boo!" He cackled as we huddled against the wall, our stomachs sick with fear. In my dreams today, an old man with a face creased and yellow from a lifetime of cigarettes hovers over me as I run through rows of unending rooms.

Nemo didn't talk about his father much. His mother ruled the household. The yellowed photographs capture a stern-faced woman surrounded by children. There are no pictures of Nemo's father. He lived part of the time in Chester, South Carolina; part in Asheville. He traveled to South Africa and South America for business interests. Jewel dealing—a shady enterprise, I thought, and imagined another family hidden away in some exotic place. He placated his domineering wife by presenting her with priceless rings and necklaces. My mother and her sisters have several of them that they bring out for weddings or funerals, but they talk of others that mysteriously disappeared.

I spent most of my time in Biggie's room, stringing beads, sewing, chatting, and playing board games. I spent little time downstairs. The black horsehair cushions stuck my bottom like pins. The heavy curtains and dark wallpaper had little appeal to a child. I avoided Uncle Arboo. I liked the kitchen where the Pekingese yelped and Aunt Annie and Aunt Nonnie squeezed lemons and added big spoonfuls of sugar to make the sweetest, coolest lemonade on Earth.

Aunt Annie and Aunt Nonnie spent their summers weeding the vegetable gardens, cooking, and cleaning. A television in the den was the only sign of the "modern world." There was no dishwasher, no garbage disposal, no washer or dryer. Sheets hung in rows south of the gardens, fluttering in the wind. We ran through the gaps between the flapping white cloths, catching whiffs of summer sun and laundry detergent. Uncle Arboo took us out to the beehives. The ominous buzzing kept us well back, but it didn't keep us from eating the thick honey and chewing on the comb.

Once a summer, Biggie took us down to the dining room. Carefully, she brought out a set of delicate bone china from the glass-front armoire. Each time, she began the story the same way, "Long ago, this china belonged to John Kennedy, my grandfather, your great-great-grandfather. . . ." She wove her Civil War tale. John Kennedy's family had given refuge to a wounded Yankee during the war—when the South was still strong. After the war, they received the elegant box of china, a touching thank-you from the Yankee whose life they'd saved.

I went back to Asheville a few years ago. By then, they were all dead and my grandmother Fufine, well into her nineties, lived in a nursing home. I searched for my childhood on that trip, thinking it might help me make sense of my present. I walked up the alley behind Fufine and Nemo's house on Tacoma Street and picked up a loose foundation brick that I keep on my bedside table. But I couldn't find the yellow house. A restaurant with a neon sign and torn screens loomed where it had once stood.

Looking Back

Memory is selective. There is much we forget or think we've forgotten. But in each of our lives, there are layers of memories, like strata in sedimentary rock. There are people and places that anchor us to our childhood, our adolescence, our grown-up years. Those from our youth are the most powerful and palpable. They shape us for better or for worse. Those incidents and feelings, fears and delights, buried deep in the recesses of memory, form the foundation of what follows. As Wallace Stegner says, "My first fifteen years were migrant and deprived, my next fifteen aspiring and academic and literary and deprived, my last fifty-odd academic and literary and not so deprived. It is progress, of a sort, I suppose; but I am still the person my first fifteen years made me."

At a recent dinner party, the conversation revealed that four of the six female guests had been raised Catholic. One of them described what a shock it was to go to college after twelve years of parochial school: "In my second month, my roommate looked at me and yelled, 'You're driving me crazy. Every morning you spend twenty minutes just standing in front of the closet. What is your problem?' I couldn't make a decision. After all those years of uniforms, it was overwhelming. 'I don't know where to start,' I told her. 'Sweats,' she said. 'It's simple. Sweats.' It didn't seem simple to me. 'But what color?' I asked her, 'Do I match the tops and bottoms?'"

The rest of us laughed.

She said, "I can laugh now, but it was traumatic. I was paralyzed. You know what else? I haven't bought anything plaid since high school. Couldn't bring myself to."

We can't escape our past. We can grow from it. We can grow beyond it. But it has shaped us and remains a part of who we are. On the mantel in my living room is a kitchen clock from the old yellow house. Every hour it chimes; every third day, I wind it, a ritual that makes me think of Nemo and his sisters. Which one, I wonder, had the job I now have of winding the clock and starting the pendulum? Who purchased it? What did the children look like then? How did they spend their days? I would like to see all that this old clock has observed. Each winding connects me to my family's history and reminds me of the passage of time in a way our battery watches or electric clocks cannot.

When we lose our moorings, when we are caught in currents beyond our control, we need to step out of the maelstrom and look back. We need to retrieve images from our youth. We need to step back so that we can leap forward. We need to take solace in that which is preserved—and somehow completed—by the gloss of memory.

Exercise: Memory

Begin by jotting down memories, little or big ones. You might want to pull out an old photo album or scrapbook or an object from your childhood to jog your thoughts. Here are some of my memories:

- I remember hitting a tree headfirst on a sled.
- I remember eating watermelon on my grandparents' back porch.
- I remember playing gin rummy with my grandfather Nemo.
- I remember spending the night at the house of the little girl next door and waking up two hours before anybody else, but not being allowed to get out of bed.
- I remember sneaking out to swim in the city pool when I was twelve.

- I remember my dad calling me "a toothpick with an olive on top" when I'd had my hair done for my first prom.

List memories as quickly as you can. Whatever appears in your mind, jot it down. It can be mundane and trivial or something that changed the course of your life. It can be joyful or full of pain. Whatever it is—how you coped with it or grew beyond it or took delight in it or laughed at it or loved it or simply remember it—it is part of what makes you who you are today. You'll be surprised at what comes to mind. Don't stop until you've listed at least twenty-five memories. This exercise puts your life in context. It helps display the panorama of your life. It unlocks your past and connects it to your present. It reminds you that life is in continual flux: Good memories mix with bad as life unfolds. What felt impossibly painful years ago has become bearable, maybe even humorous. What brought joy as a child brings comfort as an adult.

Exercise: Digression

Now read over your list. Choose one memory that you want to write about and dig in. Give this memory a context, a beginning, middle, and end. Make it rich in detail. John McPhee says about writing, you must "have the courage to digress." It is in your digressions that you will discover what you really want to say. This exercise is like an archaeological dig. It is an unearthing. It is a search for relics from your past that make you who you are today. It is a personal excavation. Any day that you feel stymied and unable to write, return to this list, select one of the memories, and write about it.

CHAPTER 8

On Paradox

The longer I work at the craft of writing, the more I realize that there's nothing more interesting than the truth. What people do—and what people say—continues to take me by surprise with its wonderfulness, or its quirkiness, or its drama, or its humor, or its pain. Who could invent all the astonishing things that really happen?

—WILLIAM ZINSSER, *On Writing Well*

DURING WORLD WAR II, MY FATHER-IN-LAW, PAUL SR., was captured by the Japanese in the Philippines weeks after Pearl Harbor. He spent the next three and a half years moving from one prison camp to another: first to Mindanao, then shuffled from Davao to Luzon to Bilibid, and then to Japan, Korea, and finally Manchuria, where he was liberated in August 1945. By the end, he weighed eighty-seven pounds.

I rifled through my memorabilia file and found the brief report that my father-in-law gave us years ago. In the quarter century that I've known him, he has spoken little about his war experience. While a prisoner on Mindanao, he worked dawn to dusk in rice paddies or sawmills. The work was long and hard, the food meager; but the guards pretty much left the prisoners alone. That situation changed suddenly, as the report, dated October 13, 1945, documents.

When he wrote his report, he was reunited with his wife Rita and was recuperating at 949 Emerson Street in Denver—blocks from the house Paul and I had bought when we settled here more than thirty years later. The report's type is blotched and fading, composed on an old manual typewriter. The description is matter-of-fact, but it is a disclosure of acts so grim and vivid in disregard for human life that they match the evil depicted in movies such as *Apocalypse Now!* or *Amistad*. In the cover memo, Paul Sr. writes:

> The attached report is an account of an abortive attempt on the part of the Japanese to remove Allied prisoners of war from the south Pacific area ahead of the onrushing attack of General MacArthur's forces. As can be seen by the date of departure (December 13, 1944), American forces were already well established on the Island of Leyte. Navy dive bombers had been extremely active around Luzon since September 21, 1944. Most of the officers who took the trip believed and still believe that the attempt was little more than mass murder. . . . The picture is not overdrawn. In many cases it is impossible to put into words the horrors and deprivations suffered by the prisoners on the trip.

On December 13, 1944, 1,619 prisoners were loaded on boats in Manila to be transported to Japan. By September 2, 1945 (Victory in Japan Day), only three hundred were alive. More than eleven hundred died on the boat; two hundred more in Japan, so weakened by the trip that they never recovered.

What is surprising is that while there were periods of unmitigated horror during my father-in-law's captivity, there were also moments of grace. Paul Sr. told us about some of them one morning as we sat around the kitchen table eating breakfast. Rita, who had not known whether Paul Sr. was alive or dead during those years, wrote him every single day. "Those letters saved my life," he said. Through the work of the Red Cross, they miraculously made their way to him, in batches with long spaces in between.

Also, each prisoner was allowed to receive one thirteen-pound package. These packages arrived haphazardly. Often weeks passed with nothing. When a parcel appeared, the men gathered around, waiting with anticipation, hoping above all that there would be food inside. A box from Rita found its way to Paul Sr. She had sent dried soups, tooth powder, spaghetti, and candy. It had taken over a year for the package to meander from the States to the prison camp. During that time most of the paper wrappers holding the foodstuffs had disintegrated. "Tooth powder was mixed with everything else Rita had sent." Paul shook his head. "The soup tasted pretty strange."

One day a package arrived for Fred Yeager, a strapping guy who had been a classmate of Paul Sr.'s at West Point and one of the best football players the academy had seen. When the parcel was delivered, prisoners gathered around Fred, all wishing for food. Fred—who years later wrote Paul Sr. that he had been hoping for canned corned beef, tuna, and coffee—opened the package and found, wrapped in paper, a deflated football.

"The last thing we wanted was a football." Paul Sr. chuckled at the memory. "We were starving and didn't have an extra ounce of energy for anything, let alone football. You should have seen the looks on those men's faces. At first they were downcast. Then they just started laughing. We were so weak that the thought of doing anything physical was hilariously ridiculous.

"Then Fred did something no one expected. I don't know what it was, frustration or hunger or sheer brilliance. He threw the football to the ground and said, 'Okay, let's play a game. Who can come up with the best recipe for cooking and eating a football?'

"It was a high point. All the men got into it. It raised morale enormously. In all my years in prison camp, that competition was one of the best moments. We laughed so hard. We forgot where we were. We were just a bunch of guys horsing around. The worst gift became the best."

We ate pancakes as Paul Sr. went on, "The conditions were terrible. We were always hungry and worn out from working in the rice fields. When we got sick, there was no medicine and no chance to rest. But the evacuation to Japan was the worst. There were three ships. U.S. Navy dive bombers sank one of them, the one with the food on it; so the Japanese captain blamed us and decided to punish us by giving us almost nothing to eat or drink. Day after day, we had rations of a half cup of uncooked rice and about six spoonfuls of soup and tea. That was when we really started losing men.

"One thing has always stayed with me from that time. It wasn't the strongest guys who survived, or the most fit or the highest ranking. It was the optimists who lived, the ones who made the decision that by God they'd get out alive. The pessimists didn't make it. You'd think it had to do with physical strength, but it didn't. It was all in our heads."

Finding Laughter in the Paradox

In *Anatomy of an Illness*, Norman Cousins talks about of the healing power of laughter. Cousins recovered from a crippling and supposedly incurable illness by working with an understanding doctor and developing a course of "humor treatment." He believed that laughter and good emotions would allow his body to heal itself. It did.

"I have learned," he wrote, "never to underestimate the capacity of the human mind and body to regenerate—even when the prospects seem most wretched. The life-force may be the least understood force on earth. . . . Protecting and cherishing that natural drive may well represent the finest exercise of human freedom."

Merriam-Webster's Collegiate Dictionary, tenth edition, defines *regeneration* as, among other things, "spiritual renewal or revival; renewal or restoration of a body or bodily part after injury or as a normal process." Regeneration is an ongoing process, if we allow it to be. After we have been seriously hurt, we are never the same. We have lost something precious. We have experienced a death.

But remember the Zen saying, "what the caterpillar calls the end of the world, the master calls the butterfly." We cannot go back, but we can go forward, stronger, more beautiful than we ever were before. Regeneration is a birthright. It is what we as humans do. It is a natural, throbbing, life-enhancing process.

Mother Earth's cycles surround us, providing lessons and proof of the flux and change that is nature's way. Death provides the mulch and nutrients for birth and growth. Without the frost of winter, there would be no buds of spring. Without the black of night, there would be no light of dawn. When our hearts are frozen with sorrow, we think that the warmth of spring will never come, but as surely as the rising of the sun, new growth will flower within us. The regenerative force is something that rests deep in our hearts. Our challenge is to access it.

Laughter can be a key, as Fred Yeager and Norman Cousins knew. Even as a prisoner of war, Fred understood the power of laughter. That football nourished the men in a way corned beef never could: It was food for their souls, erasing for a moment the grim shadow of prison camp, and renewing their spirits. Even on his "deathbed," Norman Cousins found revival through good humor. Laughter is light. It can show the way through the darkest hours. Or, as a bumper sticker that I spotted on a beat-up VW bug in Taos put it, "She [or he] who laughs, lasts."

There is the paradox that sometimes we laugh so hard we cry. It is also possible to cry so hard we laugh. As the great humorists know, there is a fine line between comedy and tragedy. It is the intense life experiences—both joyful and wretched—that move us the most. In *The Prophet,* Kahlil Gibran writes about this enigma. He says, "Your joy is your sorrow unmasked. And the selfsame well from which your laughter rises was oftentimes filled with your tears. . . . When you are joyous, look deep into your heart and you shall find it is only that which has given you sorrow that is giving you joy. When you are sorrowful look again in your heart, and you shall see that in truth you are weeping for that which has been your delight." There are certain things in life that cannot be separated. As much as we would like to shield ourselves from suffering and expand our ability to experience joy, the fact is that heartache leads to joy and joy to heartache.

We took a twelve-year-old friend of Mark's on a cross-country ski to a hut. It was a six-and-a-half-mile route, uphill all the way. At one point, Alan threw down his pack and declared he couldn't go on. We divvied up the contents of his pack and plodded forward. Later, he started crying, convinced he'd never make it to the hut. We gave him a big drink of lemonade and some food. Finally, after five hours of skiing, Alan made it. In the hut journal, he wrote, "I've never done anything this hard in my life. But now I'm here and I am so proud of myself. The hut feels warmer, the food tastes better, the friends are dearer, the sleep is deeper." Without his struggle, he never would have experienced his triumph; he never would have gotten to a place of heightened appreciation and joyfulness.

Exercise: The Best Worst Gift

Think of a time in your life when you received the equivalent of Fred Yeager's football. When you experienced something that seemed like the worst imaginable gift and you had a choice: to cry or to laugh. Write about what you did. Write about how it felt. Write about how you feel about it today. It might have started out terrible, and, with the healing gloss of time, changed. It may have remained the worst possible gift. It might continue to aggravate the heck out of you. Fine. Write about it. Fifteen minutes, nonstop.

Exercise: Blessings in Disguise

There was a front-page story in our newspaper about a woman who inexplicably lost her sight in her thirties, went on to college, and received the President's Award—the highest honor bestowed on a Metro State College graduate. "It's probably one of the best experiences I've ever had," she says. "I was blind; now I can see. . . . Now I have a better vision of the world and what's going on around me and with other people." There is truth in the phrase "blessing in disguise." Those blessings, often hidden beneath suffering and torment, bring out our true grit and force us to grow in unimagined ways. Take time to recall those you've experienced. Sit quietly. Take several deep breaths. Begin with "I never thought I could. . . ."

CHAPTER 9

Healing Places

Yes, falling in love with the earth is one of life's great adventures. It is an

affair of the heart like no other; a rapturous experience that remains

endlessly repeatable throughout life.

—Steve Van Matre and Bill Weiler, *The Earth Speaks*

WE PADDLED HARD AGAINST STRONG HEAD WINDS. The blue heron that guided us last year appeared, regal and elegant, blessing our raft and its brief time in this canyon of the San Juan River. Three golden eagles soared above. At camp, a crayfish skittered across the sand. A beaver swam upriver, felled a small tree, and played among the rocks of a rapid.

Here I listen to the rush of river and movement of branches; smell sage and piñon; bathe my skin in sun and water; find a stillness and rest in it as we sleep under stars. Our trip began with a moonless sky. The moon will reappear as we float, shedding more light, allowing me to discover the direction I must take. There are no phones ringing, no to-do lists to interfere with the river's voice. I need its counsel. Once again, I have quit a job to write, and I am not sure why.

The San Juan originates in southwestern Colorado's San Juan Mountains, craggy, snow-packed peaks that loom like visions over sage-brush terrain. Fickle and seductive, the river begins as a mountain stream, flows down alpine slopes cutting a canyon, and meanders into desert country. By the time it crosses the Four Corners area, it is sluggish and docile, thick with sediment. West of Bluff, Utah, its youth is recaptured. It tumbles in rills and rapids, a surgeon's knife splitting the Earth's skin and leaving behind clean red rock wounds that reveal 60 million years of carving, exposing the Earth's striated glory before coming to a premature end in the waters of Lake Powell, its life shortchanged by the Glen Canyon Dam. During its journey, it has sliced through twenty rock formations—from the oldest, Barker Creek Stage, to the youngest, Morrison Formation—and has displayed sedimentary rocks that date back more than 500 million years. It is an artery of life in scorching country as serene, exquisite, and inhospitable as any on this Earth.

We say we go to the desert land of the Colorado Plateau to explore rivers, buttes, and canyons. Really, we go to cleanse ourselves of daily cares and distractions, to get in touch with something that too often eludes us in our overscheduled lives. Perhaps it is the rekindling of awe; perhaps a reconnecting with a greater power. When we return home, we long to bury our feet in sand and ache to recapture the clarity of the night sky. "I need a dose of desert," one of us will say, and we start applying for river permits in January. By June, we can't stay away. It is a lover's yearning. And so, we go back and follow the rivers—the San Juan, the Green, the Colorado, the Dolores, the Chama—where they lead us.

Last year, we came to a fork at an island in the river. The current was fast and our last-minute decision misguided. We picked the wrong arm and, after floating several hundred yards, hit a stretch so shallow and rock-filled that the boat grounded. It was a brutally hot and exhausting day; we were hungry, ready to find a campsite and call it quits for the evening. But we were stuck and had no choice but to get out and push the raft upstream against a powerful current. After twenty minutes of groans and curses, we were back at the fork, able to board again and flow without a struggle. We put down our paddles and leaned back, letting the river do the work.

"We had to have learned something from that," I muttered, "but I can't imagine what."

"It's obvious," my son, Mark, quipped. "Sometimes you have to go backwards to go forward."

I think of that now, as I try to find my way to the place where I can flow again, without questions and doubts. This is my backtracking phase. I have been fighting the current, trying to make a river rushing the wrong way my own: I must go backwards to go forward. The job I left was not for me. I have fought political battles and butted my head against bureaucracies before. I have other work to do.

I think of all the years I struggled to fix Katherine, to alter the genetic course of her life. What a frantic effort it was and what a relief when finally it dawned on me that my job was not to fix Katherine, but to love her, simply love her. She would have graduated from high school this year. There would have been proms, corsages, and graduation ceremonies. There would have been cheers and accolades and great expectations for her future. And she remains immobile in her hospital bed, moved where we decide to move her, fed when we decide to feed her. We have made it through two decades, and I am humbled by Kat, by her gentleness, by her beauty, by the few demands that she places upon us. She is a flower whose smile is a blossom that sends a shock wave to the heart, and I miss her. How I wish she were floating down this river with us.

There is a distinct beginning and end on these trips—a put-in and a take-out. Once we begin, we have no choice but to complete the course. We go forward as fast or as slow as the current and our paddle arms allow. We make homes along the river: camps where we hang a clothesline, pitch our tents, set up our kitchen, wash, sleep, and wake to the desert sunrise. These places become more than home. In one night, our roots sink deep into bedrock. As we depart, we bless our camp and sense that we are leaving something sacred behind. Yet we float away more whole than before.

At night the river comes to me in dreams, always crystal blue, though the river that flows beside me is milky brown—"too thick to drink, too thin to plow"—a mixture of silt and sand, of layer upon layer of stone ground down to water, shifting, moving, altering this space. Millions of years' worth of work surround me, and I have this single moment, this fleeting friendship with a river, ancient, noble, ever changing, ever remaining the same.

We've hiked from the river to the top of the canyon rim where the land stretches, a huge flat field with outcroppings of buttes, but no sound or sign of the river below; plunged into desert pools, surprise oases in the midst of slick rock sculpture; and been awakened by a desert downpour that drenched our sleeping bags and splashed our faces.

I'm never as happy as I am here, sitting alone, listening to Earth sounds, having paddled enough to make my arms feel strong, well-used. Yet I leave the river exhausted, run down by the elements, hair encrusted with sand, and grit packed under my fingernails, wondering why year after year I go out in this lonely, godforsaken country, where dreams have been made and shattered like the oil rig we passed on the riverbank, brought a thousand miles only to smash to pieces as it fell on the last five hundred feet of its journey. Who would dare think this land could be invaded and tamed? Not even the Anasazi settled in the canyon depths. They knew powers beyond their reckoning ruled in country so exquisite, barren, and lonely. Lacking arrogance and gold dust in their eyes, they were not driven to conquer land meant to inspire poets and gods, but never, ever to be tamed.

Today the sky began and ended gray, a canopy of shade and rain to hide the desert glare. From my perch beneath a rock overhang, I watched a curtain of rain move across the cliff horizon as the rapids blasted beneath and the wind roared. When I am within these canyon walls, it's as if I've come home after too long away. I hear more and see more, and I am at peace.

Healing Places

There are places that help us heal because they share the magic of their perspective. They allow us to stand back and view our lives more broadly. They provide a place of quiet in the midst of the flurry of our commitments. A healing place might be a small café with the smell of brewing coffee. It might be a bench in a museum in front of a favorite painting. It might be a city park or a mountain trail. It might be a church with beautiful stained-glass windows. It might be a rocky beach or a desert canyon. It might be a hammock in your garden. These places speak to us in voices only we can hear. They beckon us to visit. They are different for each of us. But each of us has a healing place that we know or that is there for us to discover.

Healing places are terribly important. They remove us from our everyday bustle, if only for an hour or a day. They provide a respite from a sometimes chaotic world. They soothe our hearts and souls. These are places where we feel fuller, less frantic, more at one with the world around us. If you don't have a healing place yet, think about places over the course of your lifetime that have made you feel more at peace. It might be impossible to hop on a plane or get in the car for a long drive, so think about what is nearby: a park, a church, a library, a coffeehouse, a museum, a place that welcomes you and makes you feel simultaneously calmer and more alive.

The Newsstand Café is an unpretentious place with wooden floors, large picture windows looking out to the street, racks of newspapers from all over the country, an endless array of magazines and greeting cards. Order a latte, and you can stay for hours—writing, talking, reading. You pay when you order, and bus your own table, so there is no need for the "Can I get you anything else?" or "Would you like your check now?" interruption. There is no rushing. For $2.50, my cup is filled, and I walk away with boosted spirits.

Exercise: Your Healing Place

Write about a healing place you visit or that exists only in your imagination. How do you feel when you are there? What lessons do you take from it? How can you rearrange your life so that you can spend more time there? Begin with "When I am in my healing place, I. . . ."

Nature Mind

We live in a world where the concrete of highways and air-conditioning of malls keep the elements at bay, giving us the illusion that we are masters of nature. We live in a time when entertainment is packaged in Disney amusement parks or MTV sound bites. We program our children so that they have little time to listen to the wind or climb a tree. We pay a huge price for our isolation from nature. We become detached from rhythms and forces that have guided humankind throughout time. We lose touch with nature's cycles, which reflect the cycles of life: spring/birth, summer/maturity, fall/old age, winter/death.

Part of our healing comes from a realization of interconnectedness. In acknowledging our grief, we must understand that we have lost something precious, we have suffered a death—a literal death or a death of our dreams and expectations—but there is new life around us all the time in the natural world. There is a continual renewing that occurs—birth to death, death to birth. There is a growing and changing and dying that is constant. It is the nature of nature. It is the nature of life. It is dangerous to get too removed from nature's voice, a voice that can be benign as well as ruthless, full of beauty or destruction. It teaches us that while we have control over some things, others are beyond our reckoning.

Exercise: Your Nature Connection

Write about your nature connection, whatever it might be. Write about your view out over the Carolina marshes, that special tree in Central Park, that patch of sky you see from your window, that field of corn that spreads as far as the horizon, the tomatoes in your garden, the autumn colors in New Hampshire, the smell of the sea in Key West.

First, list sensory details: How does your nature connection smell, taste, sound, look, feel?

Second, fill in the emotional details: How does your nature connection make you feel?

Third, review your lists and write for fifteen minutes about your connection to the natural world and what it means to you.

CHAPTER 10

Sometimes Bad Is Good

Healing is embracing what is most feared; healing is opening what has been closed, softening what has hardened into obstruction, healing is learning to trust life.

—JEANNE ACHTERBERG

*I*T WAS THE LAST DAY OF A RAFT TRIP. MY SON, Mark, had a cup of hot water gripped between his bare legs. He swiveled to grab a tea bag, knocked into the cup, and sent scalding water pouring down his thighs.

I was getting dressed when I heard his shriek. It had to be a rattlesnake, I thought. When I looked out of the tent, I saw Mark dashing for the river. By the time I made my way to him, his lower body was submerged in the Green River.

Within minutes, his scorched skin turned white, and huge blisters formed. Second-degree burns covered his inner thighs. It was 7:00 A.M. We were four miles from the take-out. Moving as if we were part of a synchronized dance, we stuffed sleeping bags, packed food and utensils, folded tents, tied in our dry bags, and launched in a record half hour. We placed an ice bag from the cooler on Mark's burns, cushioned him so that the rapids wouldn't disturb him too much, and raced to Swasey's Landing. Once there, I sped to the parking lot to fetch our van while Paul and the children started to unload the raft. I searched in all three parking areas, then searched again.

"It isn't here," I panted.

"What?"

"I've looked everywhere. No van."

Paul set out to find it. Five minutes later he was back, cursing the shuttle company, which had failed to ferry our van from Sand Wash, a four-hour drive north.

We were stranded in the desert fifteen miles from the nearest phone with a seriously burned twelve-year-old and no idea how we were going to get ourselves out of our predicament. I envisioned permanent scars up and down Mark's legs, but that was the least of our worries. His pain was extreme and Tylenol ineffective. While we gave him water to soothe what seemed to be an insatiable thirst, he continued to shiver. Wrapping him in fleece jackets didn't help. Vaseline, the only ointment we had in our medical kit, seemed to make the burns worse.

After a couple of dismal hours sitting on our gear in the blazing sun—doing the best we could to soothe Mark while trying to decide whether to start the ten-mile walk into town or wait a little longer in the hope other rafters would appear—a group from Holiday Expeditions, a local rafting outfit, showed up. The guides pulled out their first-aid kit, bundled Mark in a sleeping bag, carried him to their van, and raced us to the emergency medical clinic in the town of Green River.

There we were met by a physician's assistant who had worked in the burn unit at a major Salt Lake City hospital. Within forty-five minutes, he'd cut off Mark's shorts, doused the wounds with an anesthetic ointment, dressed them, instructed us on treatment, and popped a codeine pill in Mark's mouth. By the time we left, Mark was freshly bandaged and the pain had subsided.

"Keep those legs out of the sun for a year," the P.A. said as Mark hobbled out of the recovery room. "By next summer, you won't even be able to tell you were burned." He gave Mark a handful of lollipops. "Call me tomorrow, and let me know how you're doing, okay?"

"Sure," Mark said, shaking the P.A.'s hand. "Thanks a lot!"

My daughter Alice and I helped Mark limp across the street to a hamburger joint and settled in for a long, slow meal. Still we had no car and were stranded six hours from Denver.

While I'd been at the clinic with Mark, Paul had tracked down a puddle jumper that would fly him to the tiny landing strip at Sand Wash where the van sat. When he told Barbara, the airport manager, about our situation, she immediately said, "Your kids should stay at my house. It's empty, and they're welcome. You can use my truck to get your gear."

Paul picked us all up in a 1976 Ford pickup. We crammed in, dropped the kids at Barbara's, headed to Swasey's Landing to retrieve our raft and other gear, then drove back to the airport.

"Sorry to hear about your son," said Barbara in greeting me. "You just take it easy, and make yourselves at home. There's ice cream and root beer in the fridge. We'll get Paul up to Sand Wash lickety-split."

She insisted I drive her new Pontiac—"it's easier to handle"— back to her house and leave the truck for her.

We were dirty and disheveled from six days on the river. Barbara treated us like royalty. Her random act of kindness affected our lives, turning a disaster into a pleasant interlude and a warm human encounter. Twinges of shame shot through me as I acknowledged how unlikely it was that I would have done the same if the tables had been turned. Living in a metropolitan area had made me wary and suspicious of strangers.

Paul's plane took off for Sand Wash. I returned to Barbara's and the most welcome shower of my life. Helen and Alice fixed root-beer floats and settled down to watch *Star Wars*. Mark napped on the sofa.

Later, Barbara checked in on us. Recently divorced, she was alone for the first time in years. "I knew I needed to keep busy," she said, "so I did what I've always wanted to do." By herself she had built three lily ponds and planted one hundred different types of flowers, each variety labeled. "I'm hosting a party for my twentieth high-school reunion. I'll be ready."

I remembered a teacher friend who talked about avoiding the human magnets of unpleasantness at her school. "They're energy sappers," she'd say. "I've made a pact to stay away from them." Barbara was the opposite: an energy giver with an expansive and generous view of the world. She opened her heart and her home and made us feel as if we were doing her the favor.

"Next time you're in Green River, you stop by now," she said as she left to finish up at the airport.

By 6:00 P.M., Paul had returned with the van. We wrote a note thanking Barbara for sharing her oasis with us, packed up, and headed back to Denver eight hours late, worn out and worn down, but with hearts full from having been embraced by a small town in the midst of desert country.

Sometimes Bad Is Good

Perhaps life is a journey toward acceptance, toward the belief that everything that happens to us happens for a reason. The hardships and upheavals, the losses and heartaches have a purpose in the small or grand scheme of things. Either we conclude that there is order and purpose in the universe, or we concede that all is meaningless accident. We must choose which of these outlooks will guide our lives. This may be the most important decision we ever make. It is difficult to learn to trust life, especially when life seems to play tricks on us. In the midst of a messy divorce, chronic illness, career setback, or despair over a child, it is nearly impossible to see the good in the situation. But our life challenges and losses are opportunities for us to appreciate and love differently, to drink in the smallest details of life, to celebrate what we have as we mourn what we've lost. This is part of letting go and accepting the outcome, whatever it might be. This is part of moving from hope, which can mask reality, to trust, which acknowledges the bold, sometimes bitter, facts and says yes to life.

Exercise: Lost and Found

When we are overcome with heartbreak, we forget that life still goes on and there is much that is good in our lives. We need to remind ourselves of what our lives are really like. Try this: Divide your page into two columns. At the top of the left side, write, "Losses." At the top of the right, write, "Resources." On the left, list what you have lost (a normal child, the joys of her growing up, personal freedom because of the need to care for her, grandchildren, son-in-law, confidence in life). On the right side, list what resources you have to help you cope with your loss (medical breakthroughs, supportive spouse, loving friends, other children, healthy parents, love of nature, many interests). This exercise helps put your life in perspective. Keep both lists going. Focus first on one loss and then broaden that to losses throughout your life (moving, losing a pet, dealing with your parents' divorce, your father's illness, your mother's alcoholism). For every loss, remind yourself that you have help in coping with it.

Exercise: The Silk Purse

Remember a time when everything went wrong, when you thought it simply couldn't get worse, but somehow you not only made it through, but made it through better than you'd ever imagined?

Begin with "It was one of the worst times of my life . . . ," and keep writing until you can end with "and so it became one of the best times of my life."

Trusting in Magic

I suppose it has something to do with trust, trusting that there is a reason for what life throws our way. I suppose it has to do with accepting a certain largesse, and laughing when we find ourselves in absurd and troublesome predicaments. It has to do with taking it all in—the good, the bad, the ugly. It also has to do with realizing that there is magic afoot in the world. It revolves around us, giving us signs like a much-needed tube of sunscreen floating in a desert river, or a horned owl sitting on a canyon ledge hooting at dawn. There are forces of good, and there are forces of evil; and when the good is at work it gives us gifts, large and small. Some call it coincidence. Some call it synchronicity. Some call it grace. Some call it the magic of the universe.

From a distance, I once fell in love with a cowboy singer, Ian Tyson of Ian and Sylvia fame. Every song he sang reached deep into my forty-year-old heart to a fragile, precious place that I had long kept hidden. I listened hour after hour, day after day, searching in his lyrics for the lost cowgirl within, knowing that if I could find her, it would somehow help me come to terms with Katherine. One day I was driving to work, listening to "The Old Double Diamond," an enchanting lament about the demise of a once-great cattle ranch near Dubois, Wyoming. As the car next to me sped by, I noticed its bumper sticker and simply couldn't believe what I saw: the picture of a bucking bronco and under it the phrase "I'd rather be in Dubois." Who had ever even heard of Dubois? It had to be a sign that I needed to head straight to Dubois and check it out, but the reality of four children under eleven knocked that possibility right out of me. Instead, that evening I started writing a letter to Ian Tyson. That letter grew into the first short story I'd ever written, which started me writing about my life with Katherine, which led to my book *Grief Dancers* and the writing path where I remain eight years later—all because of a bumper sticker.

In 1991 my mother-in-law Rita died of brain cancer. We adored Rita. She had been the one who bought Katherine, Helen, and Alice taffeta dresses, frilly bonnets, and patent-leather shoes every Easter, baked fifteen kinds of cookies for Christmas, and kept special slippers for each child neatly lined up in her closet. Rita had never faltered in her devotion to Katherine and treated her the same before she was hurt and after. She and Paul Sr. had shared fifty good years. We all missed her terribly, but my father-in-law's life was drastically changed.

After Rita's death, an old grade-school friend of Paul's wrote a note of condolence and invited him to lunch. Paul and Dottie hadn't seen each other for fifty years. They had gone out a couple of times in high school. Paul had left for West Point and a military career. Dottie had married and stayed in Denver. Her husband died after they'd been married seventeen years.

Paul and Dottie started going to restaurants and the opera together. An autumn love grew, and a year later they were married. Dottie has said she almost didn't write the note, but something compelled her to.

Exercise: Amazing Grace

We'll focus more on synchronicity later. But let's start thinking about it and opening our minds to it. It is a type of risk-taking. It is listening to our inner voices and being aware of the "signs" that come our way. It begins with a little tickle (I can't believe that I've been dying to put a hammock between those two trees, and I get this catalogue that has an absolutely perfect hammock on the front cover. I can't believe that I started out hiking and realized I'd forgotten my visor, and an hour into the trail, I find a sage-green Nike baseball cap. I can't believe that the woman I sat next to at a funeral in Washington, D.C., is a dear friend of my best friend in San Francisco) and ends with an opening up to the universe. Let's start with the tickle. Write about a coincidence that you can't forget. Include the details. Where were you? How did it happen? Why was it so amazing? What did you feel when you realized what had happened (or was happening)? What does it make you think about the way life works? Appreciate the moments of grace in your life.

CHAPTER II

The Power of Poetry

In a dark time, the eye begins to see.

—THEODORE ROETHKE

*T*HE HOMES IN OUR MOUNTAIN NEIGHBORHOOD
were built in the twenties and thirties as vacation homes for folks
from Denver. They started out as small log cabins—most with a
monumental moss-rock fireplace—and have been added onto
here and there over the years so that most of the houses have a
camp (as in Boy Scout) personality and bizarre floor plan. Until
the 1970s, there was no interstate and no gas station or grocery
store nearby. The first year-round settlers were a hearty breed,
undaunted by blizzards or lack of services.

The houses are clustered together and bordered by 1,200 acres
of open space, which, combined with scarce water, will keep the
community the size it is today. The roads are unpaved, rutted, and
narrow. In spring, the dreaded mud season hits, fueled by snow
melt from late-season storms. There is a loosely defined "stew-
ardship committee" that tries to prevent gross aesthetic viola-
tions, but has had no impact, despite periodic efforts, on getting
rid of the flat-tired 1940s pickup trucks, one red and one green,
that grace a neighbor's yard. When we first moved here twelve

years ago, I viewed them as junk; over the years they've metamorphosed in my eyes into pieces of historical yard sculpture.

We also have a holiday practice of sticking small gifts in neighbors' mailboxes. There's something elflike about the tradition. No one sees the presents being left. No thank-you notes are written. Often the surprises are small and edible, delights quickly consumed and forgotten. The ritual underscores a spirit of good cheer and caring during the holiday season.

One year our neighbor Maggie—a single mom who can wield a hammer like a pro and serves on the volunteer fire department—unexpectedly stopped by on Christmas Eve day. Outstretched in her hands was a basket laden with Linzer tortes, decorated with a huge pink bow, and topped with a brass French horn–Christmas ornament.

"I love this time of year," she said as she presented the basket. "Even when it doesn't snow."

"Thanks so much." I took a bite of a torte. "This is delicious. Should cheer me right up."

"Yeah?"

"This time of year is tough. I think back to our first Christmas with Katherine when we had all our hopes and dreams. We talked about how next Christmas, it would be wonderful to see her opening presents, excited about Santa."

We chatted a bit more, and when Maggie left, she gave me a hug.

Early Christmas morning, when Santa was madly rushing around doing his business, I opened the front door and found a white envelope—in it, a poem:

Kat, the Christmas Angel

Humbly, she moves among us.
Humbly, she came.

"No room at the inn," said those who saw in Mary just another
   no-account broad
With her no-account child,
Born in the straw, for want of some greater accommodation.
But wise men come, seeing the star,
With gold and myrrh and frankincense,
For purity
Celebrates
The inner light of humble packages
And the proud struggle the rest of us wrest from them
In their opening.

Have a very Merry Christmas, with much love and a little frankincense.

Your friend and neighbor,
Maggie

My Christmas blues melted before Maggie's spirit and insight. I could see Katherine as "inner light in a humble package." That gift of words allowed me to understand once again the paradox: that it is through the greatest struggle that we receive the greatest gifts. For years I had fought against that concept, not wanting it to be true, wanting to wish away the struggle part, remembering how at the height of grappling with the reality of Kat's stark future, I could see no good there, none, just a dark, unending tunnel. But time passed, and Kat and I grew older together. I came to see there was light, but I had to go through the darkness to see it.

Recently, I called Robert, a doctor friend. He has long been interested in the mind/body connection and had worked at a hospital where he encouraged patients to open up and talk about their lives. He was there to listen, not to prescribe medicine or recommend surgery. He told me the story of one woman whose chronic breathing problems landed her in the hospital every few months.

"The nurses came to me and said she was ready to talk. Betty was afraid that this time she might not make it out alive. I sat down and told her I was there to listen. When she began, it was like breaking an abscess. She spewed her guts about a lifetime of unacknowledged grief. It wasn't an easy story to sit with: It was such a hostile landscape, and she ticked off all the little landmarks along the way—pain, danger, hurt, a wretched marriage, time on welfare, children who had abandoned her. One thing after another. But by the end of the two hours, she was a different person. There was an immediate positive change when she was 'unburdened.' The nurses told me she was more relaxed, breathing easier, and had good color in her face the next day. Two days later, she was released."

The unburdening didn't always work. Other elderly patients recited their life stories—where they were born, where they had lived, gone to school, the type of work they'd done, who they had married—with no emotion whatsoever. Robert observed no changes then. It was only when the patients were willing to talk about things that had really bothered or hurt them that a weight lifted and their health improved.

Our conversation meandered as I queried Robert more about his observations. Then he made a very personal statement about the role of poetry in his life. "The thing that helped me deal with my own repressed anger was so simple, it's ludicrous. I was listening to a Buddhist monk's audiotape *Transforming Anger*. At one point, he says, 'If you're angry, write a poem about it.' What a stupid idea, I thought. But a couple of days later, Sarah, my fourteen-year-old, really ticked me off. Instead of blowing up at her, I went to another room, pulled out a sheet of paper, and wrote this:

> *Little flower*
> *beauty*
> *also has thorns*

> *I bleed . . .*
> *life*
> *We're alive!*

"Writing that poem allowed me to see the situation in a different light. My anger melted away. The poem was an unambiguous reminder that life usually involves a little pain, and, if I'm bleeding, I must be alive."

Poetry helps us relieve anger, recast sadness, retrieve appreciation. And you don't need to be a T. S. Eliot or Emily Dickinson or John Milton to write poetry. Maggie's poem gave me a different way of viewing Katherine. It illuminated my Christmas blues and transformed them from sadness to comfort. Robert's poem allowed his anger toward his daughter to evaporate into an appreciation of her and of being alive.

Nobel Laureate Octavio Paz says, "I think the mission of poetry is to create among people the possibility of wonder, admiration, enthusiasm, mystery, the sense that life is marvelous. When you say life is marvelous, you are saying a banality. But to make life a marvel, that is the role of poetry." Poetry condenses and clarifies. It soars and steadies. Often it comes through us, and we are surprised to discover what arrives on the page. When we write through our losses, we need to honor our images and memories. Poetry provides a different format for "speaking," a different vehicle for exploring what we care most about.

Each one of us is a poet, though we've been told—in many different ways—that that isn't so. Poetry is connected to breathing. It fills us. It has a rhythm and a spareness. Its compactness offers no padding. It is closer to the heart than other writing. Poetry gives us a way to capture an image, a moment, a feeling, a memory.

When Paul and I lived in Paris after law school, we exchanged language lessons with a French student, English for French. He had us spend hours pronouncing *"pur et fin et clair."* He said if we could pronounce those three words correctly, we could say anything in French. I don't think we ever got the pronunciations right, but I've thought of those words hundreds of times over the years, drifting down rivers, skiing to back-country huts on sunny days, reading poetry. *Pure. Fine. Clear.* It's what you get to when you write poetry from the heart—purity, fineness, and clarity.

The Poet Within

Lucille Clifton once said, "Poetry began when somebody walked off a savanna or out of a cave and looked up at the sky with wonder and said, 'Ah-h-h!' That was the first poem. The urge toward 'Ah-h-h!' is very human, it's in everybody." Yet it is hard to believe it is in us. We look around and say, "It's in him, or in her, or in someone else, but I don't think it's in me. Poetry scares me. No, I'm sure it's not in me." But it is, and it can be a powerful tool for dealing with images that won't leave you alone.

Exercise: Creating a Poem

Poet Georgia Heard has an exercise that creates a poem from the inside out. It is a very effective way to get started and to discover unexpected ways of observing everyday objects. First, choose something on your body; it can be a strand of hair, a toenail, a ring, a pair of glasses, a belt, whatever. Next, divide your paper into four sections:

- In one section, describe the object in as great a detail as possible.
- In the next, list all the feelings that the object evokes. Be specific.
- In the next, create similes for the object (It is like . . . It reminds me of . . .).

- In the last section, put yourself in the place of the object, take on the voice of the object, and write from the object's perspective.

Do this quickly, no more than twenty minutes for the whole exercise. This is stream-of-consciousness work. Capture your "first thoughts."

Once when I did this exercise, I focused on the necklace that I wore, and this is what I came up with:

Description: This is a silver-and-turquoise necklace. It fits my neck like skin. I never wear jewelry, but this isn't jewelry; it is my life. It represents the Southwest, the canyons, the Indians of northern New Mexico, the love of my husband who gave it to me as a gift.

Feelings: When I look at this necklace, I feel encircled, secure, beautiful, loved. I feel more me. There is something protective about it, as if when I wear it, all that is good emanates from it and from those who come near me.

Similes: It is like a desert crown, like a blue island in a silver sea, like a dog collar that identifies me.

Voice from the object: I was crafted by a Hopi Indian who knew the earth and the sky like her own breath, who was a part of the land as I am a part of the land. I was wrought from rock and stone and by wearing me, you become more at one with the earth.

This poem followed:

> *A plunge pool, silver and blue,*
> *found in the desert.*
> *This necklace dances.*
> *I am lost in it.*
> *It traps my love*
> *for canyons and clouds,*

a life companion
playing a magic flute
at the shore (crafted by winds).
There are hands on this necklace,
dark and ancient.

Now get very comfortable; read over what you've written; close your eyes and think about the images you've collected; take several deep breaths; slow down and listen to your breathing; reread what you've written one more time. Remember, you don't need rhyming couplets or iambic pentameter to write a poem. You need images and inspiration. You need anger or pain or a burst of joy. You have all of that right here, right now. Don't strive for perfection. There is no such thing. But there is a poem—in fact, many poems—waiting to find its way out of you.

Exercise: One-Line Poems

Holidays, anniversaries, birthdays can be the toughest days of all. Because they are special, they stand out. They are hard days to get through if they remind us of a changed or shattered dream. Write about the toughest day of the year for you, the day you would most like to avoid. Write one-line poems, two lines at most. Quickly. Don't think much. Give it five minutes. Here are some of mine.

- There are memories in Christmas lights whose flames won't go out.
- How can anyone have a first birthday for twenty years? Where are the milestones in each candle?
- In an Easter egg, painted yellow, aqua, green, and purple, is the love knitted by a dead grandmother.

CHAPTER 12

Value Your Dreams

Only within yourself exists that other reality for which you long. I can give

you nothing that has not already its being within you. I can throw open to

you no picture gallery but your own soul. All I can give you is the

opportunity, the impulse, the key.

—HERMANN HESSE

I DREAM OF HOUSES: OLD HOUSES, NEW HOUSES, glass houses, wood houses, stone houses, cave houses, houses under construction, houses I've lived in, houses I've moved from. The variety and eccentricity of the houses never cease. Usually the houses, even the small ones, have strings of rooms that I walk through. I open one door after another, searching for something that I never find.

I dream of moving from my mountain house to a city house— sleek, modern, elegant. At first I am full of anticipation, delighted with the move. Then an emptiness sets in; I have a gnawing sense that I've given up something precious and there is no way I can retrieve it. This dream recurs; the types of houses vary; the decor is different; the situations alter somewhat. But always I have left

95

one house to move to something better, and realize too late what I've relinquished. The sense of regret and irretrievable loss are the same.

My grandmother Fufine, my mother, and her three sisters have houses full of Oriental carpets, elegant chintz fabrics, grandfather clocks, and highboys. For my southern family, houses are more than nests. They represent who their owners are. They are both their veneers of good breeding and their palettes for artistic expression. In my mother's family, good taste is a moral issue most evident in one's house, which needn't always be spotless, but must contain gorgeous fabrics upholstered on comfortable wingback chairs and sink-into sofas.

An army brat, then a corporate brat, I had moved to nine states by the time I graduated from high school. At each place, my mother did her best to sink down roots. She bought material, sewed curtains, pulled up carpet, had floors refinished. I think her house gave her a sense of stability and permanence in an itinerant life. There were many houses in my life, and there are many houses in my dreams. The importance of houses remains strong, a vital strand throughout my upbringing. I cannot escape the power of houses. They are external manifestations of my inner world, symbols of what is going on deep in my unconscious.

Dreams speak, and I try to listen. I go through periods of drought, unable to access them, waking with a fleeting sense that I've read a good story or seen a great movie, but I can't remember any of it. The images have evaporated, and I cannot bring them back.

Sometimes I experience a deluge of dreams, night after night, motion pictures of my interior world. I have recurring dreams and dreams I can't shake. Sometimes I'm able to make sense of their symbolic language; sometimes I'm not. Nonetheless, the images stay with me.

The following is a description of a turning-point dream I had; it led me away from a path I'd mistakenly chosen to one I needed to take. I am walking in a remote, mountainous area when I come upon a large, Japanese-style house made of wood, simple and graceful. I go in without hesitating, as if I am expected there. There are abstract paintings on the wall and sleek, handcrafted vases set in nooks in the wall. There is a sense of serenity and order. An attractive older man greets me. He is tall and slender, dressed in a silk smoking jacket. We talk for a while. I am entranced by his clever elegance and feel very drawn to him. We sit down on a sofa in a room with floor-to-ceiling windows. It is bright outside, but the light doesn't make its way into the room. The man starts kissing me. At first I welcome his advances. As the seduction progresses, something feels wrong. I realize I shouldn't be there. It is as if I have walked into a trap. I push away and leave, saying I need to go to the bathroom. Instead, I walk out of the house, down a mountain path to an open meadow that stretches to the horizon. When I look back, the man is chasing me. Frightened, I run as fast as I can through the high grasses as he pursues me. At a distance across the meadow, I spot a figure. As I get closer, I see it is a woman carrying a backpack. She is lean, tan, muscular, and looks as if she has spent much of her life outdoors. A vigor and a calm emanate from her.

I run to her. "Where are you going?" I ask, then look behind and see that the man and all of my fear of him have disappeared.

"I am going to an island to climb my sacred mountain," the woman says. She keeps walking. "Come join me," she says, motioning for me to follow her. It takes me only an instant to decide. I walk quickly until I am striding beside her, looking out to an island that appears very far away.

This dream came to me at a time of great doubt. After thirty rejections, I'd decided to self-publish *Grief Dancers*. Five thousand copies had just arrived in our garage. I'd finished my writing project, I thought; it was time to reenter the world. Several people had told me about a great foundation job. I polished my resume and put my hat in the ring. The job was offered to me on my forty-fifth birthday, and weeks later—after launching *Grief Dancers* with a few readings and television appearances—I started.

Within months, I knew I'd made a big mistake. I had walked right into the Japanese house. It had looked good, and I had been seduced by what I was supposed to do, not what I needed to do. I did everything in my power to try to talk myself into loving the new job. Nothing worked. The internal dissonance wouldn't go away. After nine months, I left. I continue to hold the image of the woman walking purposefully across the open meadow, and I'm with her as we climb our sacred mountain.

Dreaming

We all have turning point dreams, if we will listen. People say, "I can't listen, because I can't even remember my dreams." But you can. If you are writing in your healing journal, you can remember them more easily, because you are in the process of opening up. With your writing, you are tapping into your unconscious, letting it know that you want to hear what it has to tell, inviting its advice.

There are rituals to help retrieve your dreams. Before you go to bed at night, say, "I will remember my dreams tonight; I will remember my dreams." Chant this over and over. Put yourself in a state of mind where you welcome the messages from your unconscious. Increase your awareness of your dreams, and they will surface. Keep your journal, a pen, and a small flashlight by your bed so that you can jot down your dreams. Record them in the middle of the night or first thing in the morning, before coffee, before brushing your teeth. Make an effort. Value your dreams, and you will start hearing them. Be patient. You will recall them, and you will be amazed at what your dreams reveal. They may puzzle and confuse at first. Keep listening. Keep jotting them down. Think about them during the day. Buy a book on dream interpretation. The dream world is rich with original and fanciful images that link us more closely to our emotions and our truth. Dreams reflect our deepest selves. Their messages are profound and illuminating. It is worth the effort.

The Jungian analyst Robert Johnson says, "The purpose of learning to work with the unconscious is not just to resolve our conflicts or deal with our neuroses. We find there a deep source of renewal, growth, strength, and wisdom. We connect with the source of our evolving character; we cooperate with the process whereby we bring the total self together; we learn to tap the rich lode of energy and intelligence that waits within."

In other words, dreams help show us the way. They are part of our healing, connecting us directly with our inner worlds. When we feel discordant and out of sync with our true selves, our dreams will speak to us. They will disclose our anxieties, our tensions, our fears, our true feelings. When we are in touch with our dream world, we are more in touch with our inner lives. If we listen to our dreams and work to decipher them, we get to know ourselves better and are better able to see what course our lives should take.

We need to value that mysterious unconscious part of ourselves that is more honest and knowing, more fanciful and vibrant than our conscious minds. We need to record our dreams and contemplate the images they give us. Carl Jung said, "The general function of dreams is to try to restore our psychological balance by producing dream material that re-establishes, in a subtle way, the total psychic equilibrium." Dreams connect us to our souls and our true selves. They are a conduit to a rich and symbol-filled world that unites us with our human ancestry. They provide a dark, artistic, fantastic, and, at times, outrageous contrast to the routine of our lives. They tell us what is really bothering us, what we've repressed, what we've avoided, what we're thinking about just below the surface. If we listen, they have much to tell us. They help give a breadth and balance to our lives.

I have a recurring dream about Katherine. I am bathing her and find out that she needs to be dressed very quickly or she'll miss her school bus, or train, or airplane. The feeling is always the same. I hadn't realized something was coming to get her. When I do, I rush to get her ready. I grab one thing after another. But the diapers are tiny, and all the clothes are baby clothes. Everything I find to dress her would fit a small baby, and she is grown up. My tension mounts as I realize she will miss her ride, and there is nothing I can do. She will miss her ride to life. She will never fit in. She will remain a baby, though she will outgrow all of her clothes. I will rush around trying to find things that fit, but they never will. I am full of anxiety. I watch as the bus, or train, or airplane pulls away, leaving Katherine behind. Though I have made giant steps in my acceptance of Kat, this dream still leaps up from my unconscious, revealing the journey I am on, reminding me of my worry and my sadness, telling me that I still have work to do.

Jung says, "The two fundamental points in dealing with dreams are these: First, the dream should be treated as a fact, about which one must make no previous assumption except that it somehow makes sense; and second, the dream is a specific expression of the unconscious." In other words, trust that there is sense in the seeming senselessness of the dream; don't bring preconceived notions to your interpretation; and accept that the dream is a message from your unconscious.

Exercise: Remember Your Dreams

Do you forget all of your dreams and wake searching for them, but come up empty-handed? Do you have no connection to your dream world? Are you not even sure it exists? Write about the absence of dreams in your life. When you wake and find yourself empty, with an awareness that you've had a dream but have no way to reclaim it, how do you feel? This exercise is an invitation to your unconscious. You are acknowledging that you value your dreams but need help remembering the messages from your dream world. Don't be down on yourself for not remembering. We all go through those periods. This exercise will help free you up to remember.

Exercise: Reawaken the Dream

It is important to reawaken the mystery of dreams that visit every life. They have much to teach us about where we are on our journeys. They are of critical value when we have suffered a great loss and don't know how to deal with it. They can tell us what we are really thinking and feeling when our conscious mind is unable to. Look through your dream journal, and write about a specific dream, one that you know has messages for you. What do you most remember about the dream? How does the dream make you feel? What do you think the dream was trying to tell you? Write about every detail. Pay attention to color, place, and your emotional state during the dream. Write in a stream-of-consciousness fashion, letting the specifics of the dream flow. Hold nothing back. Remember, "it's only a dream."

On a "good dream day," don't worry about doing another exercise in this book. Writing about your dream is the best way you can get in touch with what you are really thinking and feeling. If you have a period of active dreaming, write about as many of the dreams as you can recall. Write first thing in the morning (or even better, in the middle of the night right after you've woken from a dream). Jot down enough so that you will remember the dream, then come back to it later. More of it will return. Dreams provide an unlimited supply of writing topics and capture your imagination at its most creative.

CHAPTER 13

Bad Days

Nothing gives us a greater opportunity to break through to artistry

than conflict. It is precisely this understanding and our ability to

capitalize on conflict that will enable us to accomplish all we desire

and, in so doing, help us to appreciate and enhance the most precious

moment of our life—this moment.

—THOMAS F. CRUM, *The Magic of Conflict*

WHILE FEEDING KATHERINE BREAKFAST, I BRUSH her hair, toss dishes in the dishwasher, wipe the counters, sweep the floor, start the laundry, practice spelling words with Mark, and finally pull Kat's daybook from her backpack to write a note to her teacher.

A memo drops from the daybook to the counter. My heart sinks when I see *budget cutbacks* in bold letters and learn there will be no summer school for Katherine, or at least no transportation. No transportation means two hours of driving for a three-hour program, which means no program. For the past eleven years, summer school has included swimming, physical therapy, and outings in the community for Kat; and time for me when I'm not thinking I need to feed, change, check, or spend time with her.

Quickly, I stuff the last bite of food in Kat's mouth, give her a drink of juice, wipe her face, brush her teeth, slip her coat on, and wheel her out to her bus as *How will I manage?* echoes in my mind.

By the time I'm settled in my writing room, I'm a little calmer, but still upset with myself for coming unglued. In my scheme of things, the unexpected disappointment looms large and foreboding. I'm not sure I can handle a summer with Katherine at home the whole time. I'm fighting for my few precious hours of solitude and concentration and can't imagine how I will cope without them.

I search the bookshelf for solace, but nothing I pull out soothes my disquiet. I thought I had my act together, thought I had a support system firmly in place. But here I am in a panic because of a little change in the summer schedule.

A frenzy of phone calls to find options for Katherine yields nothing. The waiting list for residential services is a mile long. The group homes are full, and emergency situations take priority. There are few apartments in our area, and those nearby are expensive and not wheelchair-accessible. An apartment is a ludicrous idea anyway. First I'd have to find someone who would live with Kat and care for her. The obstacles are overwhelming. I'm falling apart, yet a few days ago I thought I'd achieved a perfect balance between Kat's school program and two hours of a home health aide's time every day.

When Helen, Alice, and Mark get home from school, I warn them to stay away from me. "I'm always the one who has to deal with this stuff!" I shriek at Paul. It is "one of those days" and nothing I do seems to help. A wreck, I sleep fitfully, waking in the night in a straitjacket of worry.

When It Rains, It Pours

We think we have things under control, then discover one critical piece is missing and our fragile foundation crumbles. We become unhinged. The small expectations that connect us to sanity unravel. We are in a free fall. We can't believe it and wonder what we've done to deserve it. These are the times when we need to pull back and take a breather. We need to slow down and regroup. We need to put our lives back in perspective.

I have a friend who reminds me, "Susan, yard by yard, it's hard; inch by inch, it's a cinch." Sometimes we can't handle the big, looming, impossibly difficult and overwhelming possibilities. We have to stop and take baby steps. We have to stand back, admit our vulnerability, reevaluate where we are and what we have to work with.

As it turned out, money was "found" and transportation provided for school that summer. My world didn't collapse, but my reaction to the fear of that summer told me I had serious work to do. Paul and I spent hours talking about what we really wanted for Katherine and our family. We came up with a compromise. Kat was nearly nineteen. It was time for a change. She needed more independence. We needed more flexibility. Inch by inch, we came up with a solution. She'd have her own apartment, but it would be in our downstairs. A companion would live with her, but we'd be there to help. That day of disintegration brought me down, then woke me up. It took more than a year to obtain necessary approvals and complete the building project, which included the installation of a sixty-foot wheelchair ramp, but now Katherine has her own apartment where she lives with a loving friend, Donna. I didn't know it then, but that miserable day was a call to action.

Exercise: Upchuck Writing

Go to a quiet place with your notebook, and write about everything that has gone wrong. Write about the frustrations, the aggravations, the fears, the upset, the sadness, the hopelessness. Write about how you had everything put together and then *bam!*—one thing changed and the foundation collapsed. Write about all the little things that keep adding up: Nothing is going right; nothing ever will. Vent, rage, whine. Don't think, just write. Call it upchuck writing. It's how you get it all out. Sometimes you need to unleash. You need to clear out. You can't feel better again until you do. Write about one of those days, weeks, years. Write about the combination of events that sent you over the edge. Begin with "Everything was going great and then. . . ." Fill three pages, nonstop.

Who We Are

Ancestors are citizens of the earth. They offer strength and guidance,

wisdom and understanding to those who call on them. They send

messages and comfort. They are the keepers of all the wisdom and

knowledge that came before you. The underground universe of

ancestors can ground and center you.

—DOROTHY RANDALL GRAY

GRANDMOTHER FUFINE SITS AT THE TABLE, LIFTING a fork to her mouth as the food slips from the tines. She continues to raise it to her lips, a glimmer of confusion crossing her face when the fork arrives empty. Aunt Kitty spoons a bite of mashed potatoes into Fufine's mouth. They dribble down her chin, leaving smears of white. Fufine dabs her chin delicately with a linen napkin.

We ferried Grandmother from her small room in the nursing home to Kitty's for a family meal. How thin she has become, this woman who throughout my life worried about her own—and everyone else's—"few extra pounds." She likes curry, filet mignon, chocolate mousse, whiskey cake. My childhood memories place her squarely in her kitchen, fussing over this sauce or that, scooping a taste with her finger, adding a touch more butter. She thrives on rich, scrumptious food, not what's on the nursing home's menu.

Dinner is done. We help Grandmother to the wicker chair on the porch. After dozing briefly, she sits staring into space. Where does her ninety-five-year-old mind take her? She remembers the birthdays of all thirty-seven great-grandchildren. She still has a weekly manicure and, on special occasions, treats herself to a pedicure. She sits with a stiff back, ankles neatly crossed, though she stumbles and can't walk without holding on to something or someone. She once had flashing dark eyes and thick brown hair, a gypsy spirit molded by convention into a perfect southern belle.

Kitty, Fufine's fourth daughter, is the keeper of memorabilia in our family. Around her house, hung on walls and buried in desk drawers, are old pictures and letters. On the desk, I uncover a picture of Grandmother's family and take it out to her: the handsome, swarthy father; the fine-boned, clear-eyed mother who died of tuberculosis when Grandmother was sixteen; the five delicate-faced children. Fufine points to her mother. "The picture doesn't do her justice, dahlin'. She was beautiful. Prettiest woman I ever saw. After Mother died, Daddy was quite the rogue. His second wife was younger than I was." Grandmother shakes her head.

"I remember when they took that picture; Mother made all of our clothes." The yellowing photograph preserves oversized bows, knickers, and freshly pressed details of lace and tucks, reminding me of the smocked dresses my mother made for my sister and me and then my three daughters.

Fufine's sister Alice and brother Tom, who sit on either side of her in the picture and whom Fufine raised after her mother's death, both committed suicide. I knew nothing about them until I was grown. While pregnant with my third child, I dreamed of a dark-haired girl running through a field of flowers as I followed behind. "Alice, come back," I yelled. When I woke, I knew if the baby was a girl, I'd name her Alice. I had not known Fufine's sister's name at the time. Later, on a trip to North Carolina, Grandmother thanked me. "I could never have asked," she said, "but it's a lovely name, and Alice was lovely." She told me the story that visit.

"I've missed her every day since she's been gone. A thousand times, I've asked what I could have done." Seventy years of heartbreak erupted in her voice. She showed me a picture of a pretty young woman with smooth skin and a whimsical expression. Now it is as if my Alice, high-spirited and fun-loving, is living for her great-great-aunt, who became so despondent that she went to the basement one day and hanged herself, leaving behind two young children.

My cousin Francie and I drive Grandmother back to the nursing home. Only she remains of her family's generation, blessed by nearly a century of life, cursed by the losses and sorrows of that much living. With her walker, she manages to make it back to her room. It is clean and neat and has a nice view out to the hills of western North Carolina. Pictures of family reunions from the time Francie and I were toddlers plaster the walls. Nemo's picture as a dashing young football player at Chapel Hill sits on the table by Fufine's bed. The door is open, and an old white-haired woman drifts in muttering about the worms that they put in her food. "It's okay," we assure her, escorting her out and then closing the door.

We settle Fufine in her armchair a few feet from the television and kiss her good-bye, but she, always the hostess, insists on accompanying us down the long hallway to the parking lot. With each halting step, the walker glides smoothly across the linoleum floor.

"Come back soon," Grandmother whispers in my ear as I hug her. Age and life have carved her wrinkled features well, and I am struck by her lingering beauty.

I cross the parking lot and turn to wave. Grandmother hasn't moved. She stands in her blue-and-yellow floral-print dress, watching with a look of longing I've never seen before, holding the handles of her walker so tight that I see the whites of her knuckles.

Retrieving the Past

The feeble grandmother; the aunt who killed herself; the other aunt who slowly drank herself to death; the great-grandmother who died of tuberculosis; the great-grandfather who was never the same after her death; the grandfather you adored: These people are part of who we are today, connecting us to our past—and reminding us of our own aging as we become the mother, aunt, uncle, or grandfather ourselves. Natalie Goldberg, author of *Writing Down the Bones,* says, "It is very important to go home if you want your work [or your self] to be whole. You don't have to move in with your parents again and collect a weekly allowance, but you must claim where you come from and look deep into it. Come to honor and embrace it, or at the least, accept it. . . . But don't go home so you can stay there. You go home so you can be free; so you are not avoiding anything of who you are." We look backward so that we can move forward with greater awareness and acceptance.

Every one of us has his or her story. We think our lives are dull, uninteresting, white-bread bland, but it doesn't take much looking back to realize that we all have a rich, weird, engaging past, peopled with heroes and eccentrics, encompassing moments of tragedy and moments of delight. There are times we need to plumb the past to make sense of the present. There are times we need to honor and reconnect with our ancestors and their stories.

In the preface to *Refuge,* Terry Tempest Williams's book that blends her observations of the natural world with her reflections on her mother's death from breast cancer, she writes, "Perhaps I am telling this story in an attempt to heal myself, to confront what I do not know, to create a path for myself with the idea that 'memory is the only way home.'" By retrieving the memories of her mother, she preserves her mother's wisdom and spirit, and helps heal her own grieving heart.

Exercise: Conversation with a Relative

Think of a relative who is growing old or has died. Pull out old family photographs to jog your memory. Now talk to that person. Talk about her life and your life. Talk about how his life has made a difference in your life. Ask her questions. Say the things you wanted to say growing up, but lacked the courage to say. Thank him, or bless her out. Have a free, open, uncensored conversation in which you share your deepest feelings about how that person affected your life, what gifts he gave you, what she took from you, what you miss most, what you would say to him if he were still alive, what questions you would ask, what about her life you never understood, what you remember most about her. Begin with "Today I am thinking of you. . . ."

CHAPTER 15

Taking a Risk

Every time we confront death-in-life we confront a dragon, and every time

we choose life over nonlife and move deeper into the ongoing discovery of who

we are, we vanquish the dragon; we bring new life to ourselves and to our

culture. We change the world. . . . If we do not risk, if we play prescribed

social roles instead of taking our journeys, we feel numb; we experience a

sense of alienation, a void, an emptiness inside.

—CAROL S. PEARSON

*W*HEN I DIRECTED A NONPROFIT ORGANIZATION, I took a woman to lunch who had been a big supporter. I wanted to get to know her. She was in her late fifties, handsome in a raw-boned, craggy-faced way, and dressed in a navy pantsuit and silk scarf. Over curried chicken salads, we started out talking about the organization—her early commitment, her belief in what it stood for. But before long, the conversation shifted to her life. Five years before she had gone through a very messy, very public divorce after thirty years of marriage and several children.

"He came up to me one day and said he wanted a divorce. Our kids were grown. I was looking forward to traveling all over the world with him. I couldn't believe it. It was a typical 'other woman' situation. He'd always been busy. It hadn't occurred to me anything had changed. Late nights at the office and business trips had been a way of life for years.

"I wanted to belt him between the eyes, but I was even more disgusted with myself. I'd stopped seeing. I'd gotten complacent. All those years together had slipped by, and we'd stopped developing as individuals, or I had anyway. He handled the finances, paid the bills, made our investments. I didn't even know how much we had. For a while I was in shock. I thought he'd change his mind, but when I realized that wasn't going to happen, I knew I had some work to do."

"What did you do?" I asked, expecting her to tell me about months of psychotherapy.

"It was simple, really. I made a deal with myself that I'd do something new every day. It could be something little like reading a magazine I'd never read or buying a new type of tea, going alone to the movies, listening to some of my kids' music—really listening to each word—taking a walk in a different part of town. Or it could be big like going on a safari or buying a new house. Each day, I took a risk. I stuck to it. I also learned all I could about investing and finance. I took classes and hired an investment advisor. It was a tough year, but by the end of it, I felt strong, really strong, stronger than I'd ever felt in my life."

I have another friend who stayed home to raise three kids. When her youngest was in junior high, she decided she was going to paint her house—a three-story gray stucco in one of Denver's oldest neighborhoods. She went to a hardware store and bought paint and scaffolding. Her husband told her she was crazy and there was no way she could do it. She spent the summer painting, all by herself. By August, the house was done, and she was ready to reenter the work world. She got a great job. "I was afraid," she said. "I had to paint that house first. I had to know I could do it."

A Risk a Day

In *The Tibetan Book of Living and Dying,* Sogyal Rinpoche talks about impermanence. He asks himself, "Why is it that everything changes? And only one answer comes back to me: That is how life is. Nothing, nothing at all, has any lasting character. . . . We assume, stubbornly and unquestioningly, that permanence provides security and impermanence does not. But, in fact, impermanence is like some of the people we meet in life—difficult and disturbing at first, but on deeper acquaintance far friendlier and less unnerving than we could have imagined."

Doing something we've never done before shakes us out of our comfort zone. It helps awaken us, and it builds strength, acceptance, and power. Writing is risk-taking. It is an exploration and adventure that leads us places we've never been before. It is trusting. We need fuel for our writing and our lives. We need to contemplate, and become comfortable with, change. We need to think about the fear and exhilaration we feel when we do things for the first time. We need to get to a place where we can embrace change and impermanence. We need to remember always that "if it's worth doing, it's worth doing badly." Perfectionism and self-consciousness are problems. They stand in the way of living.

In *Living in Balance,* Joel and Michelle Levey talk about viewing life as a learning expedition. "Embracing life as a learning expedition is the first step toward realizing balance. To understand this, it is helpful to understand the difference between living in your comfort zone and in your learning zone. Your comfort zone is what you are familiar with, what you already know so well the knowledge is almost automatic. Your learning zone is anything that stretches you beyond that, challenging you to learn new skills, new ways of relating." Spending time in our learning zones is essential if we are to grow. And, whether we like it or not, facing a significant loss throws us smack in the middle of our learning zone.

Sheila, a single mom, had worked as a secretary for ten years. After considerable soul-searching, she decided she wanted to be a corporate trainer. One day, a woman called and asked if she did training on telephone techniques; the trainer they had scheduled had canceled. The session was in two days. Could she lead it? "Sure," Sheila said. "I provide training on telephone techniques every chance I get." She just didn't go on to say that this was the first chance she'd ever gotten. That afternoon she went to a bookstore and spent one hundred dollars of her three-hundred-dollar fee on every book available on good telephone manners. It was Wednesday. By Friday, she was ready; the session was a solid success. Just going for it and taking the risk launched Sheila's career.

Exercise: Taking the Plunge

Write about a first, something you feared and dreaded. It can be something small, like the first time you tried to jitterbug or drove a standard shift by yourself; or something big, like the decision to go back to school and get that degree you've always wanted or, in middle age, to go on Outward Bound, a wilderness adventure program. Somehow you mustered the courage to do it or to deal with it. Write about how that felt or, if you are in the midst of it, how it feels. Write about taking on something you never thought you could handle—making a public presentation, writing a twenty-page term paper, leaving a destructive marriage, cooking a meal for thirty people, building a tree house—but you did. What was it? What made you decide to do it? What role did other people play in your decision? How did you feel before you did it? Confused? Conflicted?

Afraid? How did you feel afterwards? What did you learn from the experience? Write for fifteen minutes, nonstop.

Exercise: Five New Things

Now, sit down and list five new things you are going to do. These are "routine breakers." They can be very small, but you must do them. And they must be things you've never done before. I have a walk I take four or five times a week. Like a robot, I go the exact same route each time. Last week, I decided to try something different. I'd do the same walk, but I'd go the opposite direction. *I'm going the wrong way,* inadvertently popped into my head several times before I realized there was no wrong way. I started seeing things with new eyes: The view opened up in ways I'd never noticed; I saw the houses from new angles; I walked more slowly and observed more. We forget the feeling of liberation that comes from stepping out of the routines we create.

List the five new things. Don't make a big deal of them. But they have to be new experiences (going to a movie alone at 11:00 A.M.; stopping at a bookstore you've driven past a hundred times; not making your bed; making your bed; eating Chinese food for breakfast; getting up early and going out to watch the sunrise; reading a Danielle Steel novel). Over the course of the next week, do them.

Exercise: Writing out of the Rut

After you have done the five small routine breakers, write about them. Write how you thought of them, how they made you feel, what you thought about as you were doing them.

Repeat these exercises every few months. Make yourself take risks that move you from your comfort zone to your learning zone.

CHAPTER 16

On Letters

Statistically, the probability of any one of us being here is so small that you'd think the mere fact of existing would keep us all in a contented dazzlement of surprise.

—LEWIS THOMAS

Dear Paul,

I sit in this plane, floating above the clouds, trying to edit my next book. And my mind wanders to you. I am thinking of our lives together, thinking how well we fit together after all these years. It's been twenty-five years, a quarter century, and we have done so much living. Oddly, I feel younger than I've ever felt, more ready to adventure with you, to step into unknown places. I yearn for a couple of backpacks, full water bottles, and I'm ready to head to canyon country or ferries in the Mediterranean together. I'm ready to trek in Nepal or stutter our way through Argentina. I'm ready to spend the nights wrapped in your arms.

I think of your receding hairline, your graying hair, your

face that has no wrinkles, and the way you scrub it until it seems you will rub the skin off, but really you are just washing away the day's stresses. I think of sitting in front of the fire, sipping coffee early in the morning while the children sleep and the quiet of the house is ours to share. I remember each of your carpentry ventures—the tree house, storage shed, picnic table, playhouse— beginning or ending with a slice of a finger or a gouge in the thigh so that I've come to expect the gasp or groan, ready with Neosporin and Band-Aids. I see your expression as we start a raft trip or a hut ski or a mountain climb—that look that is most naturally you—boyish excitement, anticipation of adventure, escape from legal briefs and federal registers, much more the kid than high-powered lawyer. When you are gone and I am a crippled old crone in a nursing home, that is what I'll remember: that look on your face, that boy I came to adore.

The clouds are gray and heavy, billowing storm clouds that look like they will explode any minute. But above them is the palest robin-egg blue, stretching to eternity.

Love,
Susan

Letters

In *Inspiration Sandwich: Stories to Inspire Our Creative Freedom,* Sark writes, "Letters are chances for the soul to speak. A mood captured in the fibers of the paper, a world in an envelope which will not exist until it is opened. . . . Love letters make love stay visible. You can rub it, smell it, touch it, share it, and sleep with it under your pillow." In this Internet world, old-fashioned letters are a dying breed. While the instant communication of e-mail increases the ease of communication and cuts down on postage stamps, snail mail plays a different role. It preserves the mystery. There is a package to "unwrap," choices to make in terms of paper and ink. A lock of hair, a dried flower, or a pressed leaf can be enclosed. A dab of perfume can unlock years of memories. When you open the envelope, the letter writer is present.

My friend Kate is an expert at *le beau geste.* Enclosed with her letters might be a refrigerator magnet sporting an illustration of four cowgirls in full getup, and the slogan "Born to be Wild"; an orange plastic compact inscribed with "You Go, Girl"; or a picture of a moon goddess with outstretched arms holding a myriad of stars, stamped in silver on a piece of purple paper. When I receive a letter from Kate, her spirit reaches across half a continent, and I am embraced by her.

Never underestimate the power of a love letter. Not only is it a gift to the receiver, it is a gift to the creator: You express your heart, show your tender side, articulate what you value, and exalt in a connection with another. Love letters are medicine for the soul.

Exercise: The Love List

Sometimes we forget who and what we love. We are down in the dumps. We have the blues. And we forget how much there is to love, no matter what is going on around us. Love is a great healer—loving life, loving the people in it, loving your time on this Earth. That is not to say, be blind to the evil that exists. It is to say, acknowledge life's beauty and preciousness in spite of evil.

Make a list of one hundred things you love—snow, ice cream, snow ice cream, fires, that morning cup of coffee, wild bouquets of flowers, bouquets of wildflowers, *Gone With the Wind, For Whom the Bell Tolls,* that extra-soft flannel nightgown. Quick, list them without thinking, those little life-enhancing things that bring a smile to your face and make you feel happy to be alive. Don't stop at ten or fifty. Get all the way to one hundred. You'll think you can't, but you can.

Exercise: The Love Letter

Put your list aside, and think about someone you love. This can be someone who is alive or dead. This can be the person who helps to make your life joyful or the person you miss most in this world. Write a love letter to that person. If she is alive, send it to her. It will brighten her heart. If the loved one isn't alive, send it to someone else who also loved him. That person will remember with you.

Exercise: The Hate Letter

There are love letters, and there are the other kind. There are those letters that we need to write because we are so angry, so fed up, so frustrated, so sad. We feel underappreciated and taken advantage of. We feel abandoned, left to fend for ourselves when we were sure a friend or relative would be there to help. We feel that life has let us down or, worst of all, we feel as if we've borne the brunt of evil. These letters are as important as the love letters. And you'll know if you need to write one. The bad feelings must come out. Often, we don't even know why the pain and disappointment are so palpable until we sit down and start writing to a specific person. We never need to send our "hate letters," but we do need to write them. Otherwise, the festering continues, and the wound will never heal. Begin with "You let me down. I expected. . . ."

CHAPTER 17

Discovering the Essence

If you follow your bliss, you put yourself on a kind of track that has been

there the whole while waiting for you, and the life you ought to be living

is the one you are living.

—JOSEPH CAMPBELL

BICYCLES HUNG FROM THE CEILING AND WERE stacked against the walls. They were crammed and stuffed from floor to rafters in the narrow room. In the middle, between protruding wheels and pedals, was a path barely wide enough to walk through. One exposed lightbulb, dangling from the ceiling, lit the room, which smelled of grease, dirt, and sweat. A gaunt old man in nylon biking shorts and thin-strapped T-shirt "pardoned" his way by us, pushing a bicycle as lean and equine as he. He mounted it halfway out the door and pedaled away; the beginning, I imagined, of a long training ride out from Apt, a small commercial town in the south of France.

We made our way down the bike-lined aisle to a wooden counter where a teenager worked. Paul caught the boy's eye, pointed to the bike he'd wheeled in, laying his hand on the frame and, in fractured French, said, "It's bent. *Il ne march pas* ['It doesn't work']".

"*Ah,*" said the young man, "*oui, c'est vraiment tordu* ['yes, it's really bent']."

We added a new word to our vocabulary and described in limping French our predicament. We'd been backing up our car when we hit a stone divider. The bike had been in a rack on the back. The front sprocket was so bent that the bike couldn't be used. We were planning to be in the Luberon area only one more day. We were hoping to get it fixed right away.

What we didn't tell him was that we'd already been to one shop, a shiny new place with a slick thirty-year-old manager who told us it would take him three days to get the necessary parts, another day to make the repairs, and would cost around seventy-five dollars. We had reservations in St. Remy the next day and no time to wait around. "Is there any way we could get the repairs done quickly?" The manager had looked doubtful, then recommended that we go to another bike shop. "It's down the street and to the left. Maybe Claude can help you. *Bon chance!*"

The teenager in Claude's shop put down his tools. "*Un moment,*" he said, then disappeared. Several minutes later, a thickset grizzled man with large leathery hands came out. "Claude," the teenager said, pointing to the bike, "*c'est la* ['there it is']." Claude picked up the bike like it was a tinker toy and carried it to a stand at the end of the clutter of bikes. Mounted on the stand, the bike had the forlorn look of a wounded animal.

"*Ah, zut, zut, zut. . . .*" Claude shook his head and made a little clicking sound with his tongue. He didn't say another word. He tried to rotate the wheel. It stuck against the frame. He tried it again; no luck. He picked up a small hammer and made one gentle tap on the sprocket. Paul, the teenager, and I crowded around. I felt like I was in an operating room, waiting for surgery to begin, realizing the delicacy of the operation and fearful of its outcome. Claude kept shaking his head and occasionally let out a discouraging grunt before becoming completely silent again. For several minutes he stared at the bike. He walked around it, looked it up and down, checked it from the left and from the right. Then his head stopped shaking, and there wasn't a sound in the room.

With the precision of a clock maker, he began. He pulled the wheel down with one hand and tapped with the other, pulled again and tapped. In no time at all, the wheel could rotate through the frame. He started it spinning, and as it spun, he tapped and then tapped again and again. Throughout the operation, his concentration was complete. His face was as expressionless as that of a Zen master, and the only thing in his world was that bicycle. I watched, mesmerized by the look on Claude's face and by the rhythmic sound of the hammer hitting the metal.

It was over in a matter of minutes. At the end, when the sprocket was no longer bent and the wheel rotated effortlessly on its axle, he said, "*Voilà* ['There']."

We thanked him and called him *un bon artisan*—"a great craftsman." The flicker of a smile crossed his face. He charged us fifteen francs, about three dollars. "*Merci,*" we said, rolling the bike smoothly out as Claude nodded and went on with his work.

Concentration

We live in a society where the most revered response to "How are you doing?" is "I'm swamped" or "Not enough time in the day." It is as if being busy means we are okay and our lives are full. In fact, our lives might be so filled up that they are empty. Being busy is often a way to avoid reflection, to avoid getting to know ourselves. We fear aloneness and know we won't have to face it if our plates are kept continually full. But when parts of our life get bent out of shape, we need time and concentration to mend them.

Writing is an act of concentration and reflection. It is an act of diving into the well of our inner lives. It is a process of healing and regeneration. It cannot be done when we are thinking about the fifty errands we "need" to do. If we are committed to dealing with the truly important aspects of our lives—love and relationships, our work, our creative expression, moving through sorrow, knowing ourselves—we must subtract the distractions.

Claude was a simple bike mechanic, and he was a master, superb at what he did. Think about what it means to be a master. It has something to do with practice, concentration, passion, and being completely present. Masters have lessons to teach us about living in this moment—the only moment we will ever have. They have lessons to teach us about focus and paring back to what is essential. We need to be able to retreat from the pressures of a culture in which the motto is "More is more"—more shopping, more work, more French fries, more television, more after-school activities, more this, more that. We need to know what depletes us and what replenishes us. We need to nurture ourselves so that we have the energy to go through our grief.

What fills our cups? What soothes our anxiety? What helps us confront and accept the most difficult challenges in our lives? What gives us distance and perspective on our lives? What leaves us feeling drained and saddened? We owe it to ourselves to answer these questions, to name, and by naming to know, what feeds our hearts and minds and what starves them.

Certain people are energy givers; others are energy takers. Certain activities are food for the soul; others make us feel like we've been run over by a bulldozer. Look at your life, think about all you do, and begin a list of what is important and what is not important; what you like to do and what you are burdened doing. This is all part of the healing process, because when we have suffered an injury to our hearts, minds, or bodies, we need energy to renew ourselves.

Exercise: Energy Register

Think about those people or things that free your mind to be completely present, to concentrate and live in the moment. We can't release ourselves from all of our daily burdens. We wouldn't want to. But when the scale gets too out of balance, the result is "dis-ease." This is a list-making exercise, an ordering:

- Quickly, make a list of those things that give you energy. They can be small or large things: hugging someone you love, a walk in the park with a friend, ten minutes alone (no phone, no children, no demands), a cappuccino, a bike ride, a massage, a bubble bath, a phone conversation with your favorite cousin, reading a good book, playing a game of solitaire, doing a crossword puzzle, taking a trip to the ocean, building a shed, spending a weekend backpacking, dining with friends, immersing yourself in work that you love.
- Now, make a list of those things that take your energy away: going to Wal-Mart; holiday shopping; paying the bills; watching a bad movie; an argument with your child, husband, boss, or mother; rush-hour traffic; filling out income-tax forms; job-hunting; buying a bathing suit; making small talk at a cocktail party; doing work you hate.

Exercise: The Why of Energy

Remember, what is draining for you might give someone else energy, and what nourishes you might be the last thing in the world that someone else would want to do. That's okay. As the French say, "*Chaque a son gout* ['To each his own']." The point is to know yourself well enough to know what nurtures and what exhausts you. The point is to accept that while we all must undertake some unpleasant tasks, we also have a duty to ourselves to determine what is essential in our lives, what brings us happiness.

The Dalai Lama says, "The very purpose of our life is to seek happiness." This is not a self-centered, greedy happiness, but a happiness that arises out of a fundamental connection to other human beings and expresses itself in a compassion for others and ourselves. Think about the lists: your energy givers and energy takers. Now choose something from either list and write about it. Begin with "_____ saps my energy because _____" or "_____ gives me energy because _____." Don't stop for fifteen minutes.

By writing about what gives and takes your energy, you learn a lot about what you need to take good care of yourself. Use these as idea lists. When you have a "dry" day, come back to them. Keep writing about these topics. Keep adding to both lists.

CHAPTER 18

We Look but Don't See

When you write, you lay out a line of words. The line of words is a miner's

pick, a wood carver's gouge, a surgeon's probe. You wield it, and it digs a path

you follow. Soon you find yourself deep in new territory.

—ANNIE DILLARD

AT THE CHECKOUT A YOUNG WOMAN BAGS GROCERIES. I've noticed her before. Her teeth buck slightly. She walks with a pigeon-toed shuffle. She has a quiet, high-pitched voice. She doesn't talk while she bags. She studies each item and carefully places it in a sack. She has long brown hair that reaches midway down her back. Always clipped in it are a dozen plastic bows and barrettes, all colors and shapes, scattered haphazardly like wild flowers in a meadow, serving no purpose that one rubber band couldn't serve. She never fools with her hair. The barrettes are just there.

With slender hands, she places food items in bags, with a smile too pure for the age in which we live. She finishes with my order and stacks the groceries neatly into my shopping cart.

"I like your barrettes," I say, pushing away. She doesn't respond. I don't think she hears me.

She moves on to the next checkout stand where produce has accumulated on the conveyor belt. Quietly, she gets in her place at the end of the counter. "Paper or plastic?" she asks, and begins to separate food items and pile them in sacks with methodical concentration.

I rush on, planning our dinner menu in my head, but unable to shake the image of her long hair scattered with colorful clips and bows. Then it dawns on me that the barrettes are there for a very important reason. How dull I was not to have seen, though I have noticed her time and again. How strange that it hits me now, alone on a cold winter evening—when I will be returning to Kat and my house full of kids—and leaves me feeling as if I'd been punched in the stomach.

Someone who loves her sprinkles her hair with bright plastic every morning, not as a fashion statement, not to hold back her hair or tame her locks, but to tell everyone who sees her that though she is grown, she is a child and will always be a child. The barrettes say she is innocent. They say she is loved. They ask all who come in contact with her to save her from harm. They are her shield of protection in a world that can be casually cruel. I know that's why they are there. I realize that with a startling lucidity. It's what I would do for Katherine.

Seeing Differently

So often we look, but don't see. We notice, but don't observe. When we write, we see the world differently. Symbols and stories come to us. There are unspoken lessons and messages all around us. They help us through our own pain. They help us see the world and our place in it differently.

Where I walk near my house, there is a bank strewn with poppies in July, huge orange poppies. In the midst of the blanket of orange is one pink poppy. The first time I saw it, I stopped and stared. I'd walked by that bank a hundred times, and I'd never taken the time to observe it. I just laughed. This lovely pink poppy. I have no idea what it means. But that poppy makes me happy. Now I look for it every summer, and it is always there.

Too often we walk past. We don't stop to look. Our attention is elsewhere. We're dealing with a hundred different thoughts. We don't see the plastic barrettes of meaning or the pink poppies of beauty that adorn our lives. When we open our eyes to life, we break out of our routines and we see better, more deeply, more broadly. There is a greater array of colors. Our senses are heightened.

Exercise: Noticing

Consciously slow down. Force yourself to pay more attention. Become the observer. For a day, make yourself an aware spectator. Spend time thinking about what you see, instead of rushing on in a daze. Jot down what strikes you. This does not need to be monumental. It can be an oak tree at the end of the road or a stone house you've driven past a hundred times. It can be a sign in a shop window ("Antiques and Other Damfine Junk") or a teeter-totter at the playground. It can be the woman shuffling by the park, pushing her grocery cart filled with pop cans or the Vietnam vet who stands at the busy intersection with the cardboard sign that says "Hungry. Please help. God bless." It can be anything or anyone that you failed to really take note of before.

What did you see for the first time? What made you see it? How did it make you feel to realize you hadn't seen it before? Did it reveal anything, small or large, to you? Write about what you observed. This exercise takes us outside of ourselves. It reminds us of the bigger world beyond us and helps us see with new eyes. It reminds us that in everyday life, there are small revelations. Begin with "Today I really looked, and for the first time I saw. . . ."

CHAPTER 19

Character Traits

There is a vitality, a life force, an energy, a quickening, that is translated

through you into action, and because there is only one of you in all time, this

expression is unique. And if you block it, it will never exist through any other

medium and will be lost.

—MARTHA GRAHAM

*T*HE DAY BEFORE GRANDMA BEA—A NORTH DAKOTA pioneer woman—died at the age of ninety-nine, she chatted with Aunt JoAnne on the phone, ate three meals in her apartment building's cafeteria, finished her yearly Christmas letter, went to bed, and never woke up. I might have known that that was how she would go. She was the most pragmatic person I've ever encountered, and the least troubled.

She just *did*, with little fuss, and always created—hook rugs, needlepoint, Christmas decorations, oil paintings, water colors, wood carvings. Invariably she had a project going. She never seemed bored, never seemed to wonder why she was on this Earth. If she had bouts of depression over the course of her long life, she kept them well hidden. When her husband of sixty years died, her acceptance was so deeply entwined with the grief that her carrying on was what struck me most. She took up wood carving and taught more needlepoint classes at the senior center. She kept right on going, visiting China at ninety, where she found herself in a Beijing hotel overlooking Tiananmen Square when the 1989 uprising occurred; honing her wood-carving skills in Switzerland at ninety-four. One of the most self-sufficient people imaginable, paradoxically, she never learned to drive and, all her life, relied on public transportation and the generosity of family and friends to get her where she needed to go.

My North Dakota relatives viewed the world differently. The turmoil of the sixties passed them by. Political activism, women's lib, the civil rights movement, none of the social movements of our time seemed to intrude on their lives. Maybe North Dakota is just cold and out of the way enough that the luxury of addressing causes doesn't exist there. People's causes are clear—bringing in the crops, raising a family, making a buck against the odds. Their challenges are in their frigid, harsh surroundings. The angst of our age becomes secondary as they concentrate on family, community, the farm, hard work, thrift, taking care of whatever needs to be taken care of.

Grandmother's simplicity defined her so completely that I didn't even think of her as simple. No hang-ups, no existential malaise—she was too busy recycling, conserving, preserving. Her garden, her compost heap, the canning and saving and "waste not, want not" reality of her life vision kept all the demons away.

She was the first girl in her college class to "bob" her hair, a radical step in those days. She was, I suppose, a risk-taker, but somehow I think the real reason she cut her hair had to do with efficiency and ease, not with making a political statement. She went back to college in her fifties because her son was driving to school, and she thought it was wasteful to have just one person in the car. She was motivated more by pragmatism and thrift than by politics and self-realization. And if frugality was her driving motive (she saved used Kleenex boxes for years, stacks growing in her basement workroom; "Never know when they might come in handy," she'd say), it led to a satisfying, productive, and happy life.

She never bought a Christmas present, though each Christmas, she sent packages to all thirteen grandchildren and thirty-three great-grandchildren. She made the gifts: snowflake ornaments, cloth odds-and-ends bags, yarn dolls, porcelain angels, afghans, quilts, hooked rugs. Gifts from her hands that might have been a result of her unbending frugality, but felt like love.

Different Strokes

I was running a workshop in Dallas with people from around the country who were involved in a middle-school project. We did a writing exercise on food. Never has that exercise failed me, because never have I encountered anyone who can't connect a powerful life experience to food. It can be the memory of a grandmother's cinnamon rolls, an uncle's barbecued ribs, a friend's salsa, a Thanksgiving dinner where the turkey caught on fire, the cellulite resulting from a passion for Häagen-Dazs.

After this exercise (at lunch, by the way), one man said, "That food essay didn't do anything for me. Not a thing. I drew a blank." Everyone around the table stared in disbelief. Some of their best writing had come from that exercise. Then, I had a hunch. I asked where he was from. "North Dakota," he said. That was all I needed. That's exactly how Grandma Bea would have responded. The main meal I remember from her table was gizzard casserole, an unappetizing, but no doubt nourishing, combination of chunks of gizzard and noodles with no spices; and for dessert, cookies that had never known a hint of butter. That exercise would have failed for her, too.

The range of human behavior is infinite. We admire people for different and sometimes polar-opposite reasons—the carpenter who has no desire for pecan pie or pistachio ice cream, who has never craved a brownie or a chocolate croissant in his life, and whose work is as simple and uncluttered as a Japanese garden; the designer whose profiteroles are to die for and whose table—set with handmade (by her own hands) porcelain dishes and bouquets of flowers (from her own garden)—is extravagantly cluttered and a photographer's dream; the writer who gets up before dawn each morning and goes immediately about his work, quietly, peacefully and then, at 10:00 o'clock, has a bowl of shredded wheat; the painter who needs two caramel lattes at the corner café, several long phone conversations, a walk, a quick trip to the grocery store to pick up the camembert she forgot, before picking up a brush. What we admire most in these people is that they don't fit a mold. They do their own things. They do what works for them. They haven't become homogenized. They are their own people. Their individuality shines through. They have honored their soul needs.

Pain forces us to be different, because only we can chart our course through it; only we can discover what it is that brings us joy in the face of loss; only we can sit down and write our stories; only we can know when the miracle has occurred and we are no longer beaten down by our sorrow, but fortified by it.

Grandma Bea, a North Dakota farmer's daughter and a Depression mother, had the strengths of endurance, resiliency, thrift, and simplicity. She knew how to adapt and accept whatever life threw her way. Her wants were few, but she knew what they were; and she knew how to entertain herself—always and at no cost.

My friend Jean was telling me about her courtship. Her husband is an avid outdoorsman who has climbed all fifty-four of Colorado's fourteen-thousand-foot peaks. One of their first "dates" was a climb of Mount Massive, a giant of a peak, true to its name, in the Sawatch Range near Leadville. The weather turned bad halfway up, but Art wanted to keep going; Jean wasn't about to wimp out. They (foolishly) made it to the top in a lightning storm. After reaching the summit, Jean rushed down a couple of hundred yards, the hair on her head and arms standing on end. She felt a burning sensation and realized that the metal button at the top of her hat had scalded her scalp. By the time they made it down, she was wet, starving, and utterly worn out. Art put his arm around her, patted her shoulder and said, "Jean, you're durable."

"That was not what I wanted to hear," Jean moaned. "Durable Jean. Yuck."

She is, of course, many other things: creative, energetic, welcoming, funny. But her durability later helped her face breast cancer with courage and determination and care for a dying grandmother with love and patience.

Exercise: A Real Character

Think about someone who is totally herself or himself: that crazy aunt who kept all the cats, the friend who introduced you to yoga, the grandfather who played gin rummy, the high-school sweetheart who twenty-five years later haunts your dreams. What made them who they were/are? In your notebook, write down the name of the person you have in mind at the top, and take five minutes to list their traits of character. Begin with "He was . . ."/ "She is. . . ."

Exercise: I Am

Go stand in front of a mirror. Ask yourself who it is that stands in front of you, who it really is. Take five minutes and begin with all the things that you are: "I am [a mother, daughter, husband, friend, boss, aunt, uncle, doctor, teacher . . .]." Now take five more minutes and do the more difficult task: write down your traits of character. "I am [lazy, tired, persistent, afraid, careful, protective, a risk-taker, extravagant, careless, angry, thoughtful]." This is an exercise in identifying your strengths and weaknesses. Remember all the good things about you, as well as the things you'd like to work on. You are unique in all the world. Above all, be kind to yourself.

CHAPTER 20

When Things Shatter

Makin' it in life is kinda like bustin' broncs: you're gonna get thrown a lot.

The simple secret is to keep gettin' back in the saddle.

—TEXAS BIX BENDER

A SLENDER MAN WEARING BLUE JEANS AND A RED T-shirt cavorted between vats of molten glass and a large furnace. He stuck a long rod into the liquid, pulled it out, put it into the furnace, brought it out, blew through the hole in the rod to shape it, thrust it back in the molten glass, and repeated the process, layering colored glass on top of colored glass.

We had just walked through a display room of exquisite blownglass objects—paperweights, vases, pitchers of purple, aqua, maroon, salmon, navy, the most remarkable combinations of colors I'd ever seen. Beyond the gallery was a narrow observation area, cordoned off from the work space by a wooden rail. From there we watched the artist at work.

As the ball of glass at the end of the rod grew, the frenzy of the glassmaker increased. A marionette of movement, he stepped more quickly as he thrust the ball back and forth from the vat to the furnace, paying attention to nothing except the expanding orb.

Time stopped as his dance continued, the same back-and-forth motion over and over again, until, on one thrust, the spear with the glorious ball at the end hit the furnace's metal door and stuck there with the iron rod dangling like a flag at half mast. The glassmaker's churning stopped dead. He stood, not moving a muscle.

After a minute, he shuffled across the room, avoiding eye contact with the few observers. His face looked like a slowly deflating balloon. From behind a large wooden door, he dragged a sledgehammer and carried it to the furnace. With one stroke, he knocked the ball of glass from the door, shattering it into a thousand pieces.

"Bummer," Paul muttered. "Let's go." We left the room, spent some time browsing in the gift shop, and were just heading out the door to walk through the outdoor sculpture gallery when I turned around.

"I need to see how he's doing. I'll be right back."

In the studio, all the shattered glass had been swept away. No one would have known what had happened thirty minutes before. The glassmaker was back at work, as intense as he was before, his rhythmic movement resumed.

Keep On Keeping On

Sometimes our most precious creations break—a child, a marriage, a friendship, a business. We are shattered because our stability has been destroyed and we don't know what to do. "We've done everything right, and this is what we get for it," we complain. We're angry and dismayed, and feel fundamentally betrayed. We strive for permanence, but permanence eludes us. We are devastated and don't know how we will find the strength to go on.

Sometimes there are miracles, and the shattering can be repaired. Sometimes it can't: the cancer is too far along, the injuries too severe, the marriage too damaged. I was talking to a friend, a brilliant woman who had been a progressive superintendent of a local school district until the back-to-basics folks took over the board and pushed her out. She lost her job, ended an unhappy marriage, and turned fifty in the same year. "It's like a birth," she said. "This is the beginning of the second half of a marvelous life." When we were talking about Katherine, she also said, "Sometimes you don't have a choice. You just have to get over it."

After the glass shatters, we must sweep up the broken pieces and start again. We must "keep on keeping on." We have to allow the alchemy of sorrow to do its work: at times toughening us, strengthening us, showing us that "yes, we can survive any challenge"; at other times softening us, making us more aware of others' pain, developing our empathy and sensitivity, which allow us to connect with others at a deeper level. Carl Jung said that we experience trauma in order to know the soul, to give our lives meaning. The Dalai Lama teaches that the transformation of difficulties is a path to spiritual awakening.

Exercise: Walking on the Shattered Glass

Once again, write about how you felt when the glass shattered. Write about the numbness, the despair, the dream lost, the agony, the heartbreak. Keep writing. Remember the little things that made it harder and the little things that helped you find a way to keep going. Write about the loneliness. Begin with "I have never been so lonely or frightened in my life. . . ." Keep going.

Exercise: Sweeping Up

Where are you in the process of sweeping up the pieces and starting anew? Don't worry if the glass remains on the floor and you haven't managed the energy to sweep it up. It's okay. Everything you feel is okay. How do you feel right now? Write about it. Go for fifteen minutes, nonstop.

CHAPTER 21

Valleys

It is our inward journey that leads us through time—forward or back,

seldom in a straight line, most often spiraling. Each of us is moving,

changing, with respect to others. As we discover, we remember; remember-

ing, we discover; and most intensely do we experience this when our separate

journeys converge. Our living experience at those meeting points is one of the

charged dramatic fields of fiction.

—EUDORA WELTY

THIS VALLEY IS WIDE AND LONG. HIGH MOUNTAINS rise on three sides. To get to it, you have to go up and over Berthoud Pass, a steep route full of hairpin turns with a couple of avalanche chutes. Paul and I have driven over Berthoud since 1975, when we were summer clerks in Denver. Byers Peak, a thirteen-thousand-foot mountain with a near-perfect pyramid shape, dominates the valley. Paul and I climbed Byers that first summer in '75 and have climbed it many times since, adding children to our expeditions as the years have passed.

Our first outing with Katherine was in this valley. She was two weeks old. We put her in the Snugli and climbed Mount Nystrom, a gentle peak that gives great views of Byers and Middle Park, the old name for this huge alpine valley. Kat had thick, black hair that peeked out of the pack. She made humming sounds, almost as if she were singing to the rhythm of our footsteps. We were then full with her, completed by her.

Years later, after Katherine had changed and patterning had failed and we were caught in a despair so deep that only burying it from sight kept us from madness, we bought a small apartment in this valley. We began coming up often with Helen and Alice, leaving Kat with a baby-sitter. It was a place we escaped to, but really we were escaping from Kat. We felt free on those weekends, as if we led normal lives and the pain that gnawed so relentlessly didn't exist at all. Paul and I skied and hiked and walked, and began, little by little, to forget the image of Kat in the Snugli, the embodiment of our dreams.

Paul's parents built a house here. They left military life and the hustle and bustle of Washington, D.C., to retire to this valley. Their house looks out to Byers and sits in a stand of pines. The children played in the playhouse Paul Sr. had built for them. We grilled hot dogs and ate on the picnic table beside it. When Kat was with us, Paul Sr. and Rita brought out the down-filled couch potato for her to sleep on. "Her feet always get so cold," Rita would say, kneeling by Kat and pulling on a pair of socks and the wool slippers she'd crocheted for her.

I sit on a bed in their house, so different now that Rita is gone and the children have outgrown the playhouse. On one wall, nailed to the knotty pine paneling, is a picture of me leaning over to kiss Kat's cheek on the day we brought her home from the hospital. She wears only a diaper. Her arms stretch out, one tiny knee bends, and she stares directly at my face.

In the picture, I'm a kid myself. My hair is short and curls around my head. I wear a kelly-green knit shirt. The skirt doesn't show in the picture—flowered with a black background, a wraparound to allow extra room for my still-swollen stomach—but I remember what I wore on that September day twenty years ago as if it were yesterday.

By the time Rita was dying, we'd moved from the city to the foot-hills and sold our mountain place. Her house was, by then, our toe-hold in this valley that holds too many memories. A year after Rita and Paul Sr.'s fiftieth wedding anniversary, brain cancer killed her.

Paul and I are here again in the room we've slept in many times over the years, looking out to the roof that is covered with three feet of snow. I wonder how often I can come back. I feel like a child being knocked down by the force of ocean waves; and once down I'm unsure whether I'll be able to find my footing ever again.

Labyrinths

We go in circles. We get better. Then we're undone by a memory. We think we have put the pain behind us. Then some little object or event or picture jogs our memory, and it's as if we've made no progress at all. The pain spews, like lava, to the surface of our minds. That is the nature of memory and the nature of pain. Certain losses are ours for-ever. They are a part of us. They can be embraced, but not erased. They can, if properly understood and used, provide an unexpected source of strength by giving us confidence in our own inner reserves and comfort in the knowledge that time will ease, if not obliterate, the sorrow.

Yet it is important to spend time thinking and writing about those things that don't pass; those things that continue to bubble up to our consciousness, though we've accepted our changed life and have, in many respects, moved beyond the heartbreak. We must honor the pain that remains and explore the images that surface.

I still dream about Katherine graduating from college. It's her turn to walk across the stage and get her diploma. After her name is called, there is applause and the lights are directed at her. There is a long pause as the clapping subsides to silence. Then it becomes apparent that she can't move. She's not a normal Katherine, but a profoundly handicapped one. There is no way she can accept her diploma. I want to jump on the platform to help her, but the crowd is too thick and the stage too high.

Instead of college, Katherine got her little apartment in the downstairs of our house where Donna, a truly good woman, cares for her. I've never seen her happier. And yet, though twenty years have passed, my dream for a normal life for Kat emerges unexpectedly. I cannot control those waves of sadness and nostalgia. They are imprinted in my mind and will be part of me forever.

There is nothing linear about sorrow. The stages of grief cannot be crossed off a list—did denial, check; did anger, check; did acceptance, check—and neatly tucked away. The process is messy and has a mind of its own. Like labor. Like birth.

My friend Greg once told me about hiking in Iran. His group was crossing the Zagros Mountains. The going was slow and hot and extremely rigorous. By the third night, everyone was exhausted and grumpy. It seemed they'd never make it across. Greg complained, pointing to the distant horizon, "Look how far we have to go!" The guide who stood beside him took him by the shoulders and turned him around so that he could see the ranges they'd covered. "No," he said, "you must look at how far we've come."

Yes, we may have a long way to go, but don't ever forget about the progress that you've made, the small steps or the large steps. They mount up, even on those days when it feels like two steps forward and three back.

Exercise: Forward and Backwards

Let's take a deliberate step: Write about the one thing that is hardest for you to deal with. Begin with "I have come a long way. But I can't stop thinking about. . . ."

Awakenings

The more we are able to let go of our fears, the more we can tap into the life

force. When we are continually afraid we are not OK, we cannot tap into the

basic spiritual energy available to each one of us. . . .

—CAROL S. PEARSON

SHE WAS SHORT, HEAVYSET, AND THICK-HANDED. She wore a dirty white blouse, a long blue skirt, and ragged flip-flops. In her hand she carried brightly colored scarves with brass dangles. I spotted her up ahead on the trail and stopped. I'd encountered too many pushy salespeople in Turkey and didn't want to muster the energy to deal with another, especially walking on a small island where we thought we'd escaped the merciless merchants of Istanbul and Antalya. I turned and started back up the path.

As surefooted as a goat, she caught up with me and tapped me on the arm. "Pretty," she said, holding out her arm laden with scarves.

"Very pretty." I kept walking, trying to flee from her, realizing that I couldn't deal with her hard-scrabble existence that bordered

141

on begging. It made me think of how little she had; how each season I loaded huge, black garbage bags with our "used-up" clothing for Goodwill; and how perfectly edible food went down the disposal each evening at our house.

"You like?" She pulled out a green scarf with black fringe.

"Very nice," I said.

"You want?"

"No, thank you." I avoided looking at her and kept my head pointed straight ahead and my body moving doggedly forward. She stopped talking for a while and walked beside me. We went a hundred feet or more.

She tapped me again. "You like?" She held out a red paisley scarf with brass dangles around the edges. "Like this," she said, wrapping the scarf around her forehead so the dangles hung just above her eyes. I had to look then and saw eyes that were deep, brown, and fringed with thick lashes. Her face would have been beautiful once, but the sun's force had left it wrinkled and tough and a couple of teeth were missing.

"Very pretty," I said.

"You want?"

"No, thank you." I walked on, resolved this time to leave her behind.

Minutes later I felt someone take my hand. "Come," the woman said, gripping my hand firmly in hers. "Come."

Fear shot through me, though she didn't strike me as violent or brutal. In fact, I liked her. I just didn't want to be bothered. But I was curious, wondering what she would want to show me on a tiny Turkish island, wondering how this fit into her sales pitch. I left my hand in hers.

She led me down a steep path, clutching my fingers the whole time and muttering, "Come, I show you." Finally, we came to a small amphitheater, five rows of ancient stone benches set in a semicircle, a miniature of the great theaters we'd seen at Perge, Ephesus, and Termessus, an exquisite Lilliputian theater built so that it looked out to the open Mediterranean. "Is nice?" she said.

"Amazing," I said, sitting on the front row, trying to imagine the plays that had once been performed in such an intimate setting, realizing how vital this small theater once must have been. "Thank you," I said.

"What your name?" she asked.

"Susan," I said.

"Me too," she said. I wondered how many unsuspecting tourists she'd taken on the same tour. And I wondered how many names she had assumed. "Ah," she said, "we're sisters."

She once again took my hand, but this time differently. She held out her free arm and started dancing. I began following her steps, crossing my legs as she did, raising my arms as she did. She hummed and clapped and smiled, keeping her back and head rigid as her legs and arms whirled to the beat. On the stage of the long-abandoned theater, we danced under the sun's glare, with an uninterrupted view of the sea. I was taken back 2,500 years to a time when that theater was the island's cornerstone. For a moment, I left my modern-day existence of superhighways and megamalls and experienced the energy of that ancient place, glimpsing another way of life. But, more important, I danced, with the wind in my hair and the smell of the sea in my heart. I danced and I felt totally, completely, deliciously alive.

I bought several scarves from her. I didn't bargain or bicker about price. My daughters have worn them time and again for Halloween and dress-ups. I wish I'd bought more or given her some small gift. Maybe her name really is Susan.

Staying Open

It is easy to be immobilized by pain, to believe that our lives are over and there is nothing that can help us. We're numb, and we're convinced we always will be. Yet there are surprises around every corner. When we have been wounded, one of our greatest challenges is to move far enough out of ourselves that we advance beyond our sorrow to a place where life has flavor and can be savored once again.

In *Aphrodite: A Memoir of the Senses,* Isabel Allende writes, "After the death of my daughter, Paula, I spent three years trying to exorcize my sadness with futile rituals. Those years were three centuries filled with the sensation that the world had lost its color and that a universal grayness had spread inexorably over every surface. I cannot pinpoint the moment when I saw the first brush strokes of color, but when my dreams about food began, I knew that I was reaching the end of a long tunnel of mourning and finally coming out the other end, into the light, with a tremendous desire to eat and cuddle once again." Allende wrote her way through her despair to color, glorious gluttony, and the full awakening of her senses. Dancing for a fleeting—but eternal—moment on that Turkish isle awakened a frivolous, daring side in me that had lain dormant for years as I coped with the responsibilities of motherhood.

Near the top of Mount Evans, a peak that dominates Colorado's Front Range, there is a forest of bristlecone pines. The bristlecones are ancient, the oldest trees in the United States. They do not stand tall and proud like the Douglas fir or the ponderosa. They are short, gnarled, windswept. They have seen blizzards and fires, have been shaped by snow, wind, rain, and time. When walking among the bristlecones, time itself is present in their sculptural forms and scarred trunks. All they have witnessed and endured is evident in their remarkable shapes. They have adapted and persevered, and they are utterly stunning for it. They are old-crone trees.

They remind me of several friends: Wise women whose eyes grow brighter as their faces wrinkle and their bodies sag. Beautiful women who have weathered life's tempests and whose wounds adorn them like fine jewelry. Helene, a cancer survivor, took up painting at sixty and several years later is wildly successful, doing what she loves. "I have never had so much energy," she says. Kristine, whose husband walked out with his secretary years ago, re-created herself as a motivational speaker. "We have to grieve the little things," she says, "the lost love in high school, the death of old beliefs. When I was little, my daddy always brought me Hershey's Kisses. I grieved the day I realized my daddy and chocolate weren't synonymous." These women found the courage to reinvent themselves. They live in this holy instant. They recognized that when there was a "death," they had to awaken something new.

Exercise: First Time

There are opportunities for each of us to step beyond our usual boundaries. These "creative moments" abound if we keep ourselves open to them. We had lots of them as we were growing up. It is part of the reason we remain nostalgic about our youth, because of all the new territory we charted—first kiss, first car, first formal, first bra, first lover, first paycheck, first plane ride. Write about a time you remained open and tried something new or took an unexpected journey. This can be something you did yesterday or twenty-five years ago. How did it make you feel? How do you feel about it now? Write about what it meant to your life then and what it means now.

Exercise: Right Now

Write about what you're thinking right this minute. Start a list: My jeans are too tight; I drank too much coffee this morning; I can't get this old boy/girlfriend off my mind; I miss the way she massaged my feet; I wish my parents' business hadn't collapsed; I wish my uncle wasn't an alcoholic; I wish I had better teeth; I am happy the sun is shining on this winter day; I wish my morning hadn't started out the way it did, reading that an eleven-year-old boy had been murdered on his way to school; I wish I understood the stock market better. Go for ten minutes.

Exercise: I Want To

Now list fifteen things you'd like to do that you've never done: take a boat ride on the Seine through Paris, sing backup for Fleetwood Mac, beat Bobby Fischer at chess, climb Everest, see the Egyptian pyramids, learn to tango, ride in a hot-air balloon, see the Cirque de Soleil in Las Vegas, hike into the Grand Canyon, dance with a modern-dance troupe. Just thinking about things you'd like to do awakens you to life. And remember there is no better time than NOW to try something you've never tried before. This is an active exercise. We need action language. Begin with "I've always wanted to . . . ," and follow that opening with a verb: run, write, dance, eat, skip, bounce, race, climb, tour, etc.

CHAPTER 23

Love Costs

Love costs. It costs bravery. It costs going the distance. . . . Love means to stay

with. It means to emerge from a fantasy world into a world where

sustainable love is possible, face to face, bones to bones, a love of devotion.

To love means to stay when every cell says "run!"

—CLARISSA PINKOLA ESTES, *Women Who Run with the Wolves*

*T*HE SKY GREW DARKER. THUNDER RUMBLED IN THE distance. People in the crowd at the Botanic Gardens looked up sporadically, eating picnics, sipping wine, chatting with neighbors, unwilling to let nature take over on a night so anxiously awaited. After an eight-year silence, Phoebe Snow was performing again.

Friends had called two days before, inviting us to join them at the concert. Craig talked as though I should have known who Phoebe Snow was, but I didn't. I was of the right generation, but realized when I read the program that I'd gone to law school the year she cut her first album. The next three years I'd spent in a black hole of torts, contracts, and tax and constitutional law.

Driving from our house on Lookout Mountain, the radio reported a storm alert: five inches of rain and flash floods in Douglas County, just south of Denver. Even if the concert was rained out, at least we could meet our friends and go out for dinner.

I parked in front of 730 Josephine Street, the house we'd lived in for the first seven years of Katherine's life—through patterning and macrobiotic diets, through the births of Helen, Alice, and Mark. When the children were little, we used to walk to the Botanic Gardens' concerts. That had been more than twelve years ago.

Paul pulled up behind me as I stepped out of the car. He and I both knew where we'd park, though we hadn't arranged a meeting place. We admired the brick sidewalk he'd labored over and the two maples we'd planted when we lost a giant tree to Dutch elm disease.

"They look great." I patted a trunk. "Thought I'd feel nostalgic, but it's like we lived here in another lifetime." Hand in hand, we walked the two blocks to the Gardens. The concert was on.

Sitting on a blanket, we nibbled on grilled chicken and chilled artichoke salad. Lightning struck in the distance. Three hulking security guards in hiking boots and shorts escorted Phoebe—a big woman dressed in flowing black and brown, with ringlets of short red hair—to the stage. From the first note, I put my food aside. Her voice broke the sound barrier, flowing from octave to octave, from bass to falsetto, rushing like a brook, staggering like a drunken lover, slowing like a hot southern afternoon. One of the great voices of our time and I hadn't even known about it. Within seconds, she had us "twisting and turning, turning and twisting. . . ."

She moved through a series of blues, ballads, and rock 'n' roll, each song better than the last. In the middle of the concert, she mentioned her twenty-three-year-old daughter, Valerie, who had debuted on her new album. "She says hi at the beginning of this song. It's beautiful," Phoebe said. "I miss her so much. She's my life."

I was struck by her pride of motherhood, surprised she would talk so lovingly about her daughter in the middle of a most unsentimental concert. I found the pride of motherhood stirring, as well as a strong connection to Phoebe that went beyond her music and her enormous talent.

Throughout the concert, the sky remained threatening. As the evening progressed, the menacing nature of the clouds changed. They became a buffer to the sky, producing an unexpected intimacy, a milky gray ceiling erected to keep Phoebe's divine notes closer to the earth.

By the time Phoebe heated up with "Piece of My Heart," I knew we'd reached the grand finale. Not many people can sing that song better than Janis Joplin, but Phoebe did. She dragged it out as high, as low, as long, and as wide as she could, leaving the audience breathless. When she walked off the stage, we rose en masse and started clapping and chanting "Phoe - be, Phoe - be, Phoe - be!" hoping our enthusiasm would bring her back.

We applauded a long time. I thought she might be one of those performers who didn't do encores. But now I think she was checking to see if we deserved her gift. Finally she made her way back to the stage. We settled to the ground.

"This next song is dedicated to Valerie." The audience was completely quiet. "We showed them, didn't we, Valerie?" She chuckled.

I wondered what she meant, but chalked it up to show-biz prattle. She had mentioned Valerie several times during the concert. I imagined a young woman just out of college, starting out on her career with an amazing mother as a role model.

Phoebe went on. "When Valerie was three days old, they told me she'd never live. When she was a year old, they told me she'd never walk or talk. Well, she's walking. I'm still waiting for her to talk. Every now and then when she sees a cute guy in the elevator, she says hi. She hasn't said hi to me yet, but hey, that's okay. We showed 'em, didn't we, Valerie?"

By the time Phoebe launched into "a place called never, never land / where dreams are made," tears streamed down my face. I cried for Phoebe, for Valerie, for my friend Lynn who had adopted a daughter with muscular dystrophy, for Katherine, for myself, for the whole throbbing mass of humanity around me.

The song ended.

"God bless you," Phoebe shouted, "and may each and every one of you have twenty-three years of unconditional love."

We hugged Lynn and Craig good-bye and headed to our cars, knowing already that we couldn't retrieve the preciousness of the event that had just ended.

Back at 730 Josephine, we noticed the yard needed a good mowing. The bushes needed to be clipped. But the lights were all on. There were flowered curtains upstairs and handsome maroon paint in the entrance hall. Brass lamps showed through the living-room windows. The playhouse Paul had built for the children stood firmly in the side yard. We were tempted to knock on the door and tell the new owners that we'd lived there a long time ago and just needed a quick look. Instead, we got in our cars and headed west.

Hurt So Good

I spoke at the International Rett Syndrome Association's annual conference about the power of our daughters, of their strength to teach us about love and what is important in life. Those parents, too, had been through the despair of shattered dreams and expectations. They had seen their daughters slip away. They were left with the challenge to rebuild their lives, while carrying the trepidation that "all the king's horses and all the king's men couldn't put Humpty together again." The daughters of the people in the audience ranged in age from two years to more than forty. The parents were at varying stages of dealing with the hands they'd been dealt. But we were there, coming together from all over the country to an auditorium in Charleston, South Carolina, and we were connected. We were family. We were helping one another. We understood, each of us.

After my speech, the father of a five-year-old came up to me.

"I just have to give you a hug," he said.

We embraced. He went on. "I like what you said. It really hit home. It's been so damn hard, but I've grown up so much having Heather."

He turned to leave, then hesitated. "It hurts so good," he declared. "You know what I mean? It hurts so good."

Soon after *Grief Dancers* came out, I was a guest on a local talk show in Colorado Springs. After a lively conversation with the hosts, the phones began to ring. The first call was from Phyllis.

"Susan, I know exactly what you've been through," she began. "My granddaughter Amanda has brain tumors. She's our princess, our special baby. She had her first operation when she was two; she's had three since. Each time she goes in for surgery, we don't know what'll happen. The day before her last operation, my son called. He was getting Amanda ready to go to the hospital. I could tell he was excited.

"'Mom,' he said, 'I was out in this parking lot and found a quarter on the ground. It was dirty and bent. I picked it up, took it in, and washed it off. And you know what I realized, Mom? It has as much value as any shiny new quarter. I'll never forget that.'

"He's right," said Phyllis. "God bless you and Katherine."

The great religions of the world share the underlying precept that we grow through suffering, that suffering is a fundamental part of being human. And it is the great paradox that through suffering, and suffering alone, we come to experience our greatest joy and appreciation for life. Someone once said, "Hard things are put in our way not to stop us, but to call out our courage and our strength." If we avoid suffering, if we ignore it, if we fail to embrace it fully, we become stuck. We can't move forward. We stop growing. Our problems don't just go away. They must be confronted and worked through. That is what Phoebe Snow had done. That was why she was able to share her love for Valerie in a way that lifted the spirits and expanded the thinking of everyone in the audience that night. That is what Heather's father and Amanda's grandmother had done.

Exercise: Good Hurts

Think about the phrase "hurt so good." What does it mean to you? Have you ever hurt so good? Start a list: I hurt so good when I get a massage, go to the chiropractor, have a baby, run for thirty minutes, take a yoga class, write all those letters that have been piling up on my to-do list, clean out my closet, go to the dentist. Keep the list going.

Exercise: Why the Pain?

Spend a few minutes thinking about your list and thinking about hurting so good. Now write about one of the items on your list. Why does it hurt so good? What makes the pain worth it? I always hated it when my running buddy would look over at me, and chirp, "No pain, no gain!" I wanted to punch him in the nose, but he was right. Why was he right? Think about it. Write about it. Write for fifteen minutes, nonstop.

CHAPTER 24

Slowing Down

Problems do not go away. They must be worked through or else they remain,

forever a barrier to the growth and development of the spirit.

—M. SCOTT PECK

HE TENT LAY ON THE SAND, BROWN, TIRED, twisted. The stakes were bent and zippers suspect. This was not some shiny new product from Eastern Mountain Sports. It was a tent with serious battle scars. And I had a job to do: to single-handedly set it up. I faced the undertaking with greater trepidation than when I headed to the hospital to give birth to my first child or took the bar exam in 1977.

I was forty years old, on my first Outward Bound trip, a ten-day sea-kayaking course. I had never in my life set up a tent. I'd hiked and camped. I prided myself on being an "outdoor type," but truth be known, whenever it came time to set up the tent, I made sure I was working on dinner preparation. I knew I was deficient in that department, and I didn't want anyone else to know.

Growing up, boys changed tires, took out dead mice, and set up tents. That was the way it was. I'd long been a Girl Scout, but the main things I learned were campfire songs and how to make tuna melts. At middle age, I had gaping holes in my skills. Putting up a tent had to be at the top of the list.

It had been a long day. We had left La Paz later than planned, taken an inordinate amount of time to load up the *ponga* (the support boat), and been given a lengthy orientation on kayak safety and paddling techniques before we headed out in Magdalena Bay just west of Baja, Mexico. It was nearly dark by the time we made it to our first campsite. My arms ached, my head hurt. I thought spreading a tarp on the sand and crawling into my sleeping bag would be plenty of protection for the night.

Then one of the instructors tossed a tent my way. "Can you find a good spot and set this up?"

Not realizing the gravity of his request, I nodded enthusiastically, grabbed the dingy tent, walked around the area, found a site with some wind protection from a clump of cactus, tossed the tent to the ground, and sat, staring at the scattered mess.

I was caught.

It was a dark and lonely moment. The sun had set. The wind had picked up. The quiet of the place sunk into my bones. How could I cope? I didn't want to ask for help. The trip was barely under way, and I didn't want to disclose my inadequacies. I faced a fear I had harbored for the past twenty years: that someday, someone would expose me as a fraud. "You can't compete with a man, girl! You can't even set up a silly old tent!" It was a moment of reckoning. My palms grew cold and my mouth dry. I simply didn't know if I had it in me. I didn't know if I could figure it out, no matter how much time I had.

Finally I stood up. *If I start at the very beginning . . .* , I told myself. I smoothed the nylon out on the sand, creating a flat tent to begin with, and reasoning I could build up from there. It was an arduous task peppered with bits of despair and morsels of accomplishment, ongoing errors and consequent corrections, the discovery of broken zippers and frayed holes. By the time the others had gathered around the campfire, I was still fumbling with the tent. But I'd made a pact with myself that I could do it, if I took it slowly enough, if I concentrated, and if I, against all odds, remained patient.

My slow-motion approach worked, almost. At the end I couldn't figure out how to secure the stakes in the sand and asked an instructor for advice in that area. By then the tent was standing on its own. He showed me how to make a "dead man," to tie the tent rope around a rock or piece of wood and bury it deep enough so that it remained stable in the sand. Once I'd constructed dead men all around, the tent was as secure as it was going to get.

I suppose there have been moments in my life where I've felt more proud of myself, but none come to mind right now. I burrowed my bottom in the sand and exulted in the finished product, feeling as light and free as I ever remember—such a little deal, but such a big deal to me. I could do it. I could do whatever I needed to do, if I just slowed down and took the time.

Taking the Time

One fall I did a book tour in Houston. I arranged several television and radio appearances and readings at stores in Houston and Beaumont. I had relatives and a dear friend to visit. The trip shaped up like a dream. But there was one problem: How would I get to all of the places I needed to get to?

"Just rent a car, Sue. It's no big deal," Paul suggested.

"No way. I've heard about Houston. It's spread all over the place. I'll get totally lost."

"Get a map. That's all you need. You'll do fine."

I have an abysmal sense of direction. When hiking, I search for well-marked trails or very competent companions. I can sort of read a map, but I was sure I couldn't navigate an unknown city on my own. I didn't trust a map. I definitely didn't trust myself. And I didn't have an alternative. Either I did it, or I canceled the trip.

I headed to Maps Unlimited, picked up a Houston city map and a map of Texas, got a list of all of my appointments, sat down with the maps spread on the floor and the list to my side, red pencil in hand, and literally charted my course on the map and wrote out in excruciating detail each street name and turn. On that trip to Houston, I had to stop for directions only once.

As with setting up the tent, I did something I didn't think I could do. I conquered a huge fear, for one reason: I had to. In *The Road Less Traveled,* M. Scott Peck says, "We must accept responsibility for a problem before we can solve it."

One of the best ways to accept responsibility is to get to a place where we have to do something on our own. This is the essence of problem-solving and of rising to the occasion. Once we have found our way through it—no matter how awkward or halting the journey—we are much stronger. We know what we can do.

We think (or have been told) we can't be a lawyer, run a 10K race, write a novel, learn calculus, fix a car, cut hair, play the piano, fall in love again. Above all, we think we can't get through our grief, that we will never feel whole again. We think that life will remain gray, tasteless, and scary. Each time we break through and do something we didn't think we could do, we learn more about ourselves and our abilities to get to a place of healing that we never thought possible.

Exercise: Achieving the Impossible

Write about a time you slowed down and did something you didn't think you could do. What were you afraid of? Why did you have to do it? What did you feel like beforehand? How did you make the decision to go for it? How did you feel as you were doing it? What steps did you take to be able to do it? How did you feel afterwards?

Believing in Life's Mystery

Until we accept the fact that life itself is founded in mystery,

we shall learn nothing.

—HENRY MILLER

Dear Susan,

A year ago, I spent Thanksgiving at my brother's ranch where my aging father was dying. My daughter, Ann, had just discovered she was pregnant. She and her husband had been in California for the holiday. They returned on Sunday afternoon and drove to the ranch. Ann was extremely connected to both grandparents. When they arrived, Ann immediately went to see her grandfather. Sensing that this was the end, she whispered in his ear that she was going to have a baby and that he should tell her grandmother, who had died five years earlier, when he saw her. A half hour later he was dead.

Three summers ago, Ann's husband, Baz, planted a yellow-rose bush in my backyard, the kind you see all over Taos in May and June, blooming their hearts out. Last summer this bush had hundreds of blooms. By early July, it had gone quiet. However, on the day Baz and Annie's daughter Isabel was born, a single bloom appeared.

I have gazillions more of these stories if this is the kind of thing you are thinking of. Oh, one more.

In 1989 I was on a raft trip on the Colorado River through the Cataract Canyon. I was missing my sister Cristy, who had died of breast cancer in 1984. After her death, I had been told to pay attention to the messages that birds might bring. We hiked to the Doll's House for our solos (contemplative time alone). My place was near a huge cliff with a fabulous petroglyph of a family. I sat down on a rock, feeling lonely and wanting to be in touch with my sister. Within seconds, a small bird flew over and sat right next to me. We stayed there together for a few minutes.

Here's another. Thursday morning I went to my first-ever meeting of the Taos Garden Club. They had a wonderful slide presentation on what grows and survives well in this climate and showed fabulous gardens with colors, shapes, and types of plants I had never seen. Friday, my friends Charlotte and Larry arrived for the weekend and brought me a book, *Colorado's Great Gardens*, that shows exactly how to plant and care for dry land gardens. I am launched on my decision to create beautiful plots here at my house.

On the morning my other sister, Thea, died of breast cancer a year ago—about two minutes before she took her last breath, a deer came to the sliding glass door of her room at the hospice and looked in quietly, then turned and walked away as if beckoning her to follow. A couple of minutes later, she was dead, and the sunrise flooded her room with the golden, orange glow that it knows how best to do. I have loved this image and felt the peace of her leaving and moving on.

Whoops, now they're flowing! About a year after my mother died in 1993, I went to a luncheon for scholarship recipients and their donors at CU. We had established a scholarship fund for Mom, and I was there representing the family. Afterwards I drove up Flagstaff Mountain to Gross Reservoir and went to the place where my parents had lived happily for nearly twenty years after my father's retirement. We had scattered my mother's ashes there. I sat in my car in the stillness of the mountains, and suddenly three large blackbirds began swooping around. I smiled, thinking of Cristy, Aunt Gladys, and mother, all three dead. Shortly I turned the car around and started driving slowly on the dirt road. One of the blackbirds followed me for quite a while. I knew it was my mom.

That one brings tears. Let me know if you need any more.

Love,
Betsy

I mention to Betsy, a sixty-two-year-old dynamo who lives with a chronic blood disease and family breast-cancer curse, that I am working on a chapter on synchronicity. Three days later, I receive her note. While reading it, the phone rings. It's my friend Eileen, home after a trip.

She dives into the conversation. "You won't believe what happened right before I left. I was so looking forward to a quiet afternoon with Sandy [her ten-year-old]. We'd gone to the basement to pull out the old sewing machine. Sandy had been bugging me for weeks to teach her how to sew. When we were downstairs, I heard the front door open. I'd forgotten to close it all the way. Both dogs were out. Sandy and I rushed upstairs. We saw them running away, sped to the car, and followed them. Each time we thought we had a chance of cornering them, they got away. But we could see them. At the park, this guy driving a water truck helped us; everywhere we went people tried to catch them, but it was hopeless. Both of us were crying. We knew they'd get hit. I was driving around the neighborhood with all four car doors open, yelling at those idiot dogs. Two hours, we chased them. I didn't know what to do. My plane was leaving in an hour and a half. I had to get to the airport. We round a corner and there's this cute red truck with pictures of dogs all over it. A woman gets out of the truck, kneels down, holds out a handful of dog treats. Curry and Daisy go right to her like that was their plan all along. It was a *dog food–delivery truck*. Can you believe it? I'd never seen a dog food–delivery truck in my life, and there it was, right when I needed it."

"Eileen," I say. "You won't believe it. I just started a chapter on synchronicity."

The Presence of Grace

We've all had experiences like this, where we feel some higher power is looking out for us. We didn't deserve it, but there it is. The stars have lined up, and we had nothing to do with it. Some call it grace; some call it synchronicity; some call it serendipity; some call it a connection with the divine; some call it coincidence; some call it luck. If we stay open to life, unexpected gifts begin to appear. It can be as simple as a big smile from the grocer on a frantic day or an unexpected call from an old friend the day after you've dreamed about her. It can be a chance meeting on an airplane that leads to a great job or a high-school reunion that reignites an old love. It can be sitting down at the hairdresser's, picking up a magazine, and opening it to that article you've been searching for, or hearing a word for the first time and then hearing it three times in the next two days. It can be a rose blooming to signify the birth of a first grandchild or a dog food–delivery truck at the right place at the right time. It can be something very small, but magical; or something very big, and magical. Often we don't even realize we've asked for help or a sign or a message, but the universe surprises us by intervening on our behalf.

Last spring break, my family and I backpacked for four days in Grand Gulch, an area in southeastern Utah laden with Anasazi ruins. The weather held, the ruins—kivas, cliff dwellings, arrowheads, pottery shards—were extraordinary. With three children and the need for warm clothing in case a storm blew in, Paul and I had planned everything to the last bite, committed to carrying not one extra ounce. A couple of days into the hike, we realized a bag of granola and a dozen tortillas had been left in the car, each of us thinking the other had brought them. Our slim pickings became alarmingly meager.

The afternoon of the day we discovered our food shortage, we ran into three female college students on the trail. "Everything has been perfect," one said, "except we brought way too much food." Paul and I exchanged a glance. The conversation continued until we parted with a strong feeling of camaraderie, a hefty bag of couscous, and several dried soup mixes. Their donation saved us from a very hungry hike. But the story wasn't over. When we arrived at the trail head to pick up our car two days later, the three women were just hiking out. They'd planned to hitchhike twelve miles to their car in truly remote country, where passing vehicles were few and far between. Instead, they piled into our van and we drove them to their car. The circle was complete.

Our dog, Freckles—a stray who appeared on our doorstep eight years ago on the day we buried Paul's mother, Rita—was hit by a car last June, shattering her pelvis. Because of the timing of Freck's arrival in our lives, we always viewed her as an embodiment of Rita's spirit. The vet did all she could to put Freckles back together again, but for two months, all Freck could do was scoot herself around dragging her back legs. The chance of her ever walking again grew slimmer as weeks passed with no improvement. By September, we'd given up all hope, but decided we'd give her one more month. If by October, she was still horribly crippled, we'd put her down. On Katherine's twentieth birthday, September 2, Freckles got up on all fours and walked across our deck. Within a month, she was running. Rita had always had a special love for Katherine, and I know this was her birthday present to all of us.

The world works in mysterious ways. These types of events happen to everyone. We just need to be aware of them. We need to make note of them. We need to record them, because by doing so we are honoring magic at work. We are opening our lives to grace, and we are affirming something holy. We especially need this aware-ness when our hearts have grown heavy with grief and the world appears monotone. They are little miracles—small, unexpected gifts that add color—and they are there for each and every one of us.

Exercise: Gifts of Grace

Write about your experience with serendipity, defined in *Webster's,* tenth edition, as "the faculty or phenomenon of finding valuable or agreeable things not sought for." Write about all the details leading up to it and how you felt when it happened.

Okay, you're sitting there thinking, *I've never had anything remotely serendipitous happen to me.* That's not true. Keep thinking. Once you remember one such event, you'll remember another. Jot down what comes to you. Start keeping track of them. As you do, more and more serendipitous moments will grace your life.

Exercise: Affirmation

My friend Rosa Mazone had a card printed with this reminder on it: "I am a . . .

precious	*whole*
wondrous	*sacred*
special	*total*
unique	*complete*
divine	*entitled*
rare	*worthy*
valuable	*deserving*

. . . person."

Rosa hands out her cards liberally. Think about her affirmation list. Read over it several times. Understand that you are that wondrous person, complete and deserving. Go through the list and choose one of the adjectives and write about yourself: "I am precious because . . ." or "I am wondrous because . . ." or "I am special because. . . ." What pops into your mind? I am precious because I am a child of the universe, my mother's daughter, a mother, a good friend, a wild dancer, a great gardener, a lousy singer. . . . Keep the list going. When you begin to view yourself as all of these things, the world expands for you in unexpected ways.

Taking Care

In this world without quiet corners, there can be no easy escapes . . . from

hullabaloo, from terrible, unquiet fuss.

—SALMAN RUSHDIE

MARGARET CALLS. "I HAVE PNEUMONIA. I'M BEAT, but I have two grant proposals due this week. I'm flying to Tucson to run a conference Saturday morning. Sam is having trouble in school, so I need to talk to his teachers. I cleaned the house, returned phone calls and e-mail. I tried to sit and read, but I couldn't stand it. I'm overwhelmed with guilt. I'm exhausted and frantic. I have this internal war going on: How sick is sick? I feel like I need to throw up thirty times before I can legitimately stay home."

Each spring I get a similar call from Margaret. One year it's shingles; the next bronchitis; the next strep; the next pneumonia. She pushes herself until she collapses, gathers her forces, pushes herself until she collapses, and the cycle goes on. Her marriage is rocky; her teenage son can't cope with life; she's unhappy with her job. And she can't ever seem to slow down. Is it because by slowing down she would have to confront the underlying causes of her dissatisfaction and deal with them?

Many of us treat ourselves as Margaret does. We rush and churn and create chaos, because stopping is too frightening. We fear the void, the quiet, the solitude, the loneliness. Sogyal Rinpoche says, "We are terrified to look inward, because our culture has given us no idea of what we will find. . . . In a world dedicated to distraction, silence and stillness terrify us; we protect ourselves from them with noise and frantic busyness. Looking into the nature of our mind is the last thing we would dare to do."

But there is a different way. Our losses give us the opportunity to find it. Because they are frightening and difficult, they stop us in our tracks. The world rushes on, but we're frozen. Thawing can come as we develop a new relationship with ourselves. If we slow down and take the time to listen to our true voice, we are able to discover a loving, compassionate friend within. We need that friend desperately, especially during the trials of our lives. Dealing with tragedy is a solitary journey that drains and depletes. Other friends can help, lovers caress, faith support, but in the end, we have to find our way through the pain alone. More than ever, during the tough times, we need to take care of ourselves so that we will have the strength to take care of everything else *and* the wisdom to stop sweating the small stuff.

Clarissa Pinkola Estes puts it this way: "Wild Woman will hold us while we grieve. She is the instinctual Self. She can bear our screaming, our wailing, our wishing to die without dying. She will put the best medicine in the worst places. She will whisper and murmur in our ears. She will feel pain for our pain. She will bear it. She will not run away. Although there will be scars and plenty of them, it is good to remember that in tensile strength and ability to absorb pressure, the scar is stronger than skin."

But how do we gain the pluck to take care of ourselves and listen to the Wild Woman (or Wild Man) who, too often, is locked deep inside? It is a courageous act. It is much easier to act the martyr, to say I can't take care of myself because work needs me or my children need me or my spouse needs me or whatever needs me. But there is a reason the preflight instructions tell you to put the oxygen mask on first, before you help your child.

The quiet times in our lives are refueling stations. We need them, like we need air and water, especially in this world of more conveniences, but less time. Nurturing ourselves forces us to shift from exploring outer space to exploring inner space. And it is in those internal depths that we find fortitude and gratitude: the wherewithal to weather the storms of life. This is tough in a culture that honors busyness above everything else, where the turmoil and guilt that Margaret faces are the norm.

After Erma Bombeck found out that she was dying of cancer, she thought about how she would have lived if she had her life to live over again and wrote, "I would have gone to bed when I was sick instead of pretending the earth would go into a holding pattern if I weren't there for a day. . . . There would have been more 'I love you's.' More 'I'm sorry's.' . . . But mostly, given another shot at life, I would seize every minute . . . look at it and really see it . . . live it . . . and never give it back. . . . Let's think . . . about what we are doing each day to promote ourselves mentally, physically, emotionally, as well as spiritually." In other words, let's live it, really live it while we have it. Let's take care of ourselves so that we keep growing mentally, physically, emotionally, and spiritually. Let's not allow ourselves to get so caught up in the crazy chaos of this world that we lose touch with what is really important. Let's grieve our losses and cherish our blessings.

"Easier said than done," you mutter. Yes, but it can be done, if you make nurturing yourself a way of being, a habit, a vital part of how you live. I send out an e-mail alert to a small group of extraordinary women. "How have you cared for yourself?" I ask. Each has experienced major life losses: incest, domestic violence, alcoholic parent, divorce, breast cancer, chronic illness, childlessness. Each has come through the flames with a richer patina. Each has moved from surviving to thriving. Though their lives are very different, they share a common thread: Each has learned to enjoy her own company and to take care of herself. Each has adopted habits of self-nurturing. Here are some of their responses.

First and most important for my self and for my psyche, I walk. I am addicted to it, and depend on my solo walks to soothe my soul, force me to breathe deeply, and push my thoughts out of their usual ruts. When my father died of alcoholism, I was four months pregnant, and I walked myself out of much of my grief. I pulled back a bit from my friends and family, and left the house daily for long walks around the neighborhood. For some people, running attains a Zen-like quality, but walking does it for me. It gives me an immediate attitude adjustment. When I broke my leg and couldn't walk for three months, I was truly depressed for the first time in my life, because I had no outlet for my pain. I will never take walking for granted again.

You'll think this is nuts, but I also bake when I'm sad. Chocolate-chip cookies, brownies, anything with a wee bit of chocolate to pick up my spirits. There is nothing like fresh-baked brownies to make me feel the world is not such a bleak place after all! It's like eating a hug. That's another thing I seek out when I'm in pain: lots of hugs from my kids and Stephen and my friends. There's simply nothing better or more curative for me than a hug.

Lastly, I write through the pain. It helps me enormously to sit at my computer and vomit out all the grief that is pent up in my heart. When it's too soon for me to talk about it with you or Stephen or my mom, I write it out. I couldn't talk about my dad for the longest time without sobbing, so I put all that sadness on paper, which didn't mind my constant tears. I felt as though people thought I should be over my grieving period for my father long before I was (though that was probably more my deal than theirs), and the writing gave me an outlet for the constant ache in my heart, for the guilt I felt for not preventing his death.

I told you of my big need to get the strength to move on in my life, and ask for a divorce, by going to Minnesota Outward Bound School in 1979 for a two-week women's canoeing course. That was a huge commitment to myself. I had to tell myself I was worth it. I even got called midway through. One of the kids was sick. But I didn't go home. I had to stick it out. It was the first time since having four children that I did something for myself and it enabled me to do major things, like quit smoking and leave a truly terrible marriage. It changed my life.

Small things that I do for myself to revive energy are to stay in bed and read on a Sunday morning (this seems like the most amazing way to spend time) or have a massage, which I started doing soon after I was divorced. I will have a few friends over for dinner and cook something really wonderful. Cooking is comfort for me. Even though I live alone, I cook well for myself—fajitas, bread pudding, grilled swordfish. After eating, I always say, "Thank you. That was delicious." Out loud. To the universe. I also go for long walks in the sage and look at the sky for the changing weather and seasons.

How interesting to contemplate how I take care of myself—something I've learned after years of putting everyone first. The things that come to mind are quite obvious, at least to me. First, I exercise. Exercise is sacred to me. If there is time for nothing else, I will do even a half hour of something. I also get manicures, massages when I can. When I'm very busy with work and need a change of pace, I'll call one of my kids. That is always a pick-me-up. And, I sit down at my sewing machine to quilt. I create something wild and crazy and beautiful and forget everything else that is happening. The three things that bring me the greatest joy (and in very different ways) are being with the grandchildren, being outside (particularly on my bicycle), and sewing. Soul food. All three.

immediate reflexive response:

> breathe
> breathe deeply
> tell others to breathe deeply
> ski more

second reflexive response:

> thinking about caring
> for me it is a balance
> of self-care/other-care
> of work/play.
> fortunate that my work
> is other-care.
> don't know how work
> works for others.
> please let me know.

Before I even finished reading your message, I thought of the "Inner Child Cards," a set of tarot cards ("Inner Child Cards: A Journey into Fairy Tales, Myth and Nature," Isha Lerner and Mark Lerner) I got about five or six years ago, when I was really starting into the worst stage of figuring out my childhood and dissolving my marriage. Using these cards seemed to be the most soothing and comforting thing I could do for myself, and even now, at times, it still is. The set consists of a full set of cards and a hardback book, which has excellent descriptions of each card and contains a wealth of information about the fairy tale and myth, which is used in a very positive and imaginative way to tell the story of the cards. This tarot set has done me as much, if not more, good than many thousands of dollars' worth of psychiatric care.

Also, writing letters—to a good friend—always has been and still is something that I turn to when I need to do something for myself. And, of course, reading (something I really love, like *Jane Eyre* or *All the Pretty Horses*), and listening to whatever music seems to hit the right chord at the moment. Exercise is a way I take care of myself on a regular basis, although sometimes it becomes a little compulsive (I should say used to become a little compulsive; my exercise compulsion is definitely declining along with my hormone level). I love a massage or manicure, but you have to plan those ahead, and the timing isn't always right. If the weather is right, I'll take a moon bath. And right up there with the tarot cards is an Arby's jamocha milkshake. Fortunately, I did not drink them on a daily basis when I was going through my time of trials, or things would have gotten even worse!

Caring for ourselves is a personal matter. What works for one person might not work for another. We need to discover for ourselves what soothes and rejuvenates. But there are common threads: letting Mother Nature nurture; connecting with others; creating—a quilt, delicious meal, painting; expressing—a poem, letter, story; exercising—walking, running, skiing, biking; pampering ourselves physically. There is nothing better for me than a deep, hot bubble bath in a candlelit room with Ray Lynch's *Deep Breakfast* playing. One of my outdoor buddies who is going through a difficult divorce gets out on a trail, feels the wind and the sun on her face, and has "conversations" with people who are no longer here, whom she misses terribly, but who soothe her anxiety. "I move from the outside to the inside, to spirits and nature. When I do this, it makes the world feel broader, more warm and kind. I'm no longer afraid."

Taking care is a state of mind. It does not take lots of time or lots of money. It does take a commitment to yourself, a recognition that you are worthy. It is a love song to yourself, a celebration of being alive. When the going gets tough, you need to be rocked in your own tender arms. Those arms will keep you healthier and will give you the strength to heal.

Replenishing

At a Rett syndrome conference we did an exercise in which on one side of a page, we listed all of the things that we did for others and on the other side of the page, we listed all of the things we did for ourselves. Needless to say, the do-for-others list outweighed the do-for-ourselves list about ten to one. In fact, several people in the room started crying when they saw their lists. For the first time, they realized why they were in a state of chronic exhaustion. They gave, gave, gave, and gave some more, and never replenished themselves.

In *Refuge,* Terry Tempest Williams recounts a conversation with her mother who is dying of breast cancer. "Why are we so afraid of being selfish? And why do we distract and excuse ourselves from our own creativity?" Terry asked.

Her mother replied. "It's easier. We haven't figured out that time for ourselves is ultimately time for our families. You can't be constantly giving without depleting the source. Somehow, somewhere, we must replenish ourselves."

While we are in the thick of our pain, our doubts, guilt, anger, fear, and dismay consume us. We are beaten down and will remain so after the shock of the tragedy, if we are dealing with a chronic problem—a handicapped child, financial woes, dissolving marriage, ongoing illness. If we can come to rely upon and love ourselves as we grapple with our sadness, the nature of our struggle changes. We develop a trust in life, no matter what is thrown our way. And we come to trust ourselves, to know that we will have the strength and love and compassion and humor to persevere. There is a reason for the phrase "initiation by fire." Once we have walked through the flames alone, we can handle anything. But we have to get through them, and we need all the strength we can muster to do it.

Exercise: Doing for Yourself and Others

Divide a page into two columns. At the top of one column, write, "All the Things I Do for Others" (feed and water the dog, grocery-shop, cook meals, take out the trash, clean the house, change the oil, put on the snow tires, make the bed, neaten the kitchen, help the kids study, edit school essays, mow the lawn, go to work, etc.). Start at the very beginning of your day. You'll be shocked at all you do. List every single thing you can think of. Keep both a "routine" (everyday, ongoing tasks) and an "extraordinary" (tasks you do less frequently, but probably take more time and energy) list. At the top of the other column, write, "All the Things I Do for Myself" (brush your teeth, exercise, take deep baths, read, go to movies, have dinner with friends, call your mother, clean a closet, neaten a drawer, etc.).

Exercise: Things I'm Going to Do for Myself

How did your lists come out? They should be fairly evenly balanced. Usually they're not. If they are, congratulations, you're taking care of yourself. If they aren't, begin a new list of "All the Things I Am Going to Do for Myself." In this list, include things that you will do routinely (ten minutes of deep breathing, a daily twenty-minute walk, fifteen minutes for writing every day, eating delicious foods like fresh strawberries or melon, stopping once a week for a cappuccino at your favorite bookstore, etc.) as well as extraordinary things that you will do for a special treat (a weekend in the mountains or at the beach, a massage, a half day in bed in pajamas with the Sunday *New York Times,* a day alone at a museum).

CHAPTER 27

Endings

Sorrows are our best educators. A [person] can see further through a tear

than a telescope.

—LORD BYRON

FEBRUARY 1999. ANNA'S RED-TINTED HAIR, HIGH-heeled boots, and quick wit belied her condition. I expected a bald head and sickly pallor and wondered what I would say to someone who was dying. Nan had invited me to dinner to meet her. "You'll love her." But I was apprehensive. I didn't fear Anna; I feared my reaction to her. What would I say? What would it feel like to sit beside a woman my age who has fourth-stage cancer and no hope of recovery?

Perhaps it was Nan's cozy living room with fire blazing; perhaps it was because we knew we had too little time, but I think it was Anna's cut-to-the-chase attitude. We settled into overstuffed chairs and quickly shed our protective layers. We shared stories about surviving breast cancer and dying from it; handicapped children; daughters who try to kill themselves; destructive affairs; marriages that unwind; fighting and overcoming obesity; buying a spanking-new red Volkswagen bug; wearing a black leather jacket from Goodwill, red T-shirt, and narrow black slacks to an interview for leading time-management seminars—and getting the job. Our stories encircled and intertwined, creating a fabric that bound us together as we snacked on spinach pizza and sipped white wine.

"After a training session, this guy came up to me and said, 'You're the prettiest dead woman I've ever met,'" Anna told us at one point; and later, "I didn't pay taxes for 1997, because I thought I'd be dead, but I keep waking up alive. Death and taxes are supposed to be inevitable, but look at me." Then she laughed, a deep, guttural chortle.

She seemed funny, energetic, normal, except that she was very cold, though the fire roared and the heat pumped. Nan fetched a blanket, draped it over her shoulders and upped the thermostat.

Anna had noticed changes in her breasts, a little seepage, nothing startling, but enough to make her schedule a doctor's appointment. "It didn't seem like a big deal. I thought I was being overly cautious. Several days after I went in, I got a call from my doctor. He gave me six months, over the phone. Can you believe it?"

"You should have killed the jerk," Nan volunteered.

"When was that?" I asked.

"October 1997. October is always a bad month. It's when Tara tried to kill herself. It's when I walked out on Jeff. It's when Jeff's mom died. We fall in the fall." Anna pulled the blanket tighter around her.

"It's interesting what you learn from something like this. It showed me who my real friends are. The first person I called. . . ." She looked down at her hands folded in her lap. "I was bawling. And this friend said she was really sorry, but she had eight calls to return; it would be an hour or so before she could get back to me, but she'd be happy to see me if I could come over to her house later that evening. The second person I called, who I didn't think was as good a friend—we'd worked together a bit and I'd always felt a connection—said, 'Stay where you are. I'll be right over.' Boy was she there. She took me to every single chemo treatment, sat by me, holding my hand while all those poisons flowed into my body, drove me home.

"The odd thing is how I met her. She'd called me seven years before, out of the blue, asking if I could help her find a job. I was swamped, but talked to her for twenty minutes. I needed to, but I had no idea why. Several years later we did a little work together."

"Amazing," I said. "You both knew."

"I guess love was there all along. We just didn't realize it for years."

"How do you *really* feel about the cancer?"

"It's annoying. Sometimes things get very dark. Mainly it's annoying."

"What gets you down?"

I expected her to say the physical pain or the fact she wouldn't see her daughter grow up, or the fear of the unknown. Earlier she'd mentioned the baldness: "When I lost my hair, I wore a wig for one day. I couldn't handle it. I asked my friends to get me those little caps, and that's what I wore. When my hair had grown back half an inch all over, that's when I started crying. And I started going without a cap. I heard people whisper 'dyke.' Others made fun of me. I never said anything to them. I figured I wouldn't waste my energy on people who had so much to learn.

"You know what gets me down?" She frowned. "It's people like my friend Claire: She's an executive secretary and hates her job; she has a fourteen-year-old daughter she chauffeurs every place; her husband is going to night school, so he's never around, and when he is, he's useless. Claire feels completely trapped. Bitter. I'm dying, and I have more joy in my life than she does. It's like she's dying inside, and I'm dying outside, and it's real clear to me which is worse. That's what really gets me."

January 2000. Anna has outlived her doctor's prognosis by two years. We sit in the Newsstand Café, drinking decaf lattes and eating cinnamon rolls. Already Anna has brought together a group of friends, her "family of choice," for a farewell ceremony that she presided over in a flowing gold caftan and bedroom slippers. The drugs aren't working anymore; the cancer has spread to her liver and bones. But she made it to Y2K, a personal goal. And her daughter will graduate from high school this spring.

She wears black jeans, a gray knit shirt, suede jacket, and those high-heeled boots. Her face glows with sweat, as if she has just come from the health club, but she hasn't. It's snowing outside. She's very thin. "It's getting even more annoying. My back hurts. I just bought some Metamucil, like an old lady."

"How can you look so great?"

"Yeah, thanks." She flings back her head and raises her arms in a model pose. "You know what's kept me alive. My family of choice. Connecting with people, knowing there are people out there who'd do anything for me and I'd do anything for them. I call it 'energy of heart.' I've gotten all this energy, beautiful energy, from them."

"You've given it, too."

"Maybe. Just don't confer sainthood on me. I knew I couldn't do it alone."

I'm pumping her for lessons, trying to squeeze meaning from her shortened life.

"What else have I learned? Okay. Don't just read about taking time for yourself. Do it *now*. Don't wait. When you take care of yourself, you're not being selfish but sensible. A car with no gas can't make it up the hill. You need to keep yourself filled up. It's the little things that matter. If you need to go to the bathroom, go. If you want your coffee heated up, do it. The other things can wait. Take care of yourself now."

I've gobbled my whole cinnamon bun. Anna has taken a couple of bites. She has to head to the doctor's. As she walks out, I notice the plants thick in the picture window and the pink and white icicle lights that hang from the ceiling. Already I miss her. It seems Anna always leaves first.

March 2000. We're having another gathering: Six of Anna's friends meet every couple of months for an early dinner and catch-up-on-life conversation. Anna hasn't arrived yet.

"I'm stuck," I gripe. "I'm writing this piece about Anna, and I can't capture her. I can't express what it is about her that's so amazing. I've put it down for two weeks, and I know I have to get back to it. But it's like a critical piece is missing, and I don't know what it is."

Nan, our hostess, jumps in. "I had another friend who died of cancer six months ago. Brain cancer. It took ten years, and she just got more and more self-absorbed. It was a disaster from start to finish. The bitterness. She couldn't see beyond her self and her illness. I remember thinking, 'Just shoot me. Don't let me die like that.' And then along comes Anna. She couldn't be more different. She's come to terms with the essence of living every day. All this be-here-now stuff. She really does it."

"She cuts to what's important," Sally interjects. "She doesn't futz about the past or what's going to happen down the road. The past is gone, and she doesn't have much down-the-road time left, so she doesn't dwell there. She's right here, right now. She says she's totally unafraid of death. The weird thing is, I believe her."

The doorbell rings. Anna enters, completely bald now, wearing her black jeans rolled up at the bottom, a turquoise sweater, black tennis shoes. When she sits next to me, I see more. On her smooth head are all these stickers, bright pink, blue, purple, and green diamonds. "I stopped by a Hallmark store and had to have them." She smiles. "And look at these." She pulls up her jeans and displays hot pink socks with a "Boop, boop, boop, boop, e doop" inscription and pictures of Betty herself.

"You're something, girl!" I squeeze her shoulder, and think, *Here she is buying stickers to decorate her head; she's taking a tough situation and turning it into color and play; she has totally accepted herself; she looks so damn beautiful; and she's dying.*

We sit back and wait for Anna's update, the ritual start for all of these gatherings.

"I've had three rounds of chemotherapy. My last yesterday. At the end of the month, I'll have a body scan that'll tell me how it's worked. Then I'll know if I can be here a little longer."

"How're you feeling?" Nan asks.

"I'm tired, but the chemo's much better. Last time it was horrible. It was like a colony of bugs invading my body, making everything prickly and awful, and afterwards my world felt grayed down. I was afraid it would dull down everything. But that hasn't happened. I have lots of sunshine this time."

I remembered an earlier conversation when Anna told us about a training she did for eighty managers. No one had told her they were from the company's Mexican division and didn't speak English. She stepped into the conference room and saw that they had on headsets and were hooked up to a translator who was in a glassed-in area at the back of the room. She'd tell a story. There would be a pause for the translation while she waited, and then—finally—they'd laugh or nod their heads and she'd go on.

"That must have been freaky."

"No, it was great. I love the unknown. I love figuring something out and making it work."

And here she is staring the final unknown in the face and making her own death work. She made the choice that she's not going to let it get her down, and it hasn't.

"I know who I love, and I do work I love. That's all. I don't spend much time thinking beyond that." A born teacher, she has made dying her ultimate class.

If Only

Set in cold, gray Amsterdam, the movie *Character* paints a grim picture of human nature. Through struggle, sacrifice, and self-absorption, the bastard son of a powerful bailiff becomes a lawyer. The bailiff, who we first see evicting a dying woman from a rat-infested tenement by carrying her bed out into the rain and dumping her into the mud, forces himself on his housekeeper, impregnating her. In silence, she leaves the bailiff's home and has the child alone. For the rest of the bailiff's life, he tries to persuade her to marry him. She refuses, year after year.

Watching the movie, I kept saying to myself, *If only*. If only the bailiff had spoken one word of tenderness to the housekeeper. If only the bailiff had acknowledged his son when he was young. If only the housekeeper had shown the boy that she loved him. If only the boy— now a young man—had told the attractive woman in his office that he cared for her. If only at the end the bailiff had told his son that he was proud of him, proud of what he'd overcome. If only, if only, if only. Pride, silence, and the inability to express love doomed the housekeeper, the bailiff, and the son to lives of quiet sorrow. A couple of if onlys would have changed the tragic end of the movie, and the lives of the characters would have unfolded differently.

Perhaps more than anything else, Anna has taught me that life is too fragile and too precious for if onlys. None of us has much time, but no matter what our circumstances, we have choices. We don't have time for pride, silence, and the inability or unwillingness to express love. We just don't. Period. We can choose to live our lives one way or the other. We can choose to approach our deaths one way or the other. We can shed light or we can contribute to the darkness. We can be miserable, or we can decide that whatever our life situation—even if we are dying or someone we love is—we can choose to light a candle.

A couple of weeks ago, Helen, Alice, and I saw the world premiere of *The Laramie Story*. We were trying to get last-minute tickets to *The Winter's Tale,* but not a seat was available. *The Laramie Story* was showing, and there were plenty of tickets. Did we really want to see a story about the Matthew Shepard murder: a gay college student brutally beaten and left to die tied to a fence post in Wyoming? Surely it would be vile and depressing. How could such an evil deed be made into a play? It would be a real downer. We already knew the end of the story. But we were curious.

Over the course of the evening, the play turned a tragedy into art. Matthew could not retrieve his life, but his death took on more meaning. No longer was it a senseless and purposeless murder, but a death that had the potential of opening hearts and reducing intolerance. Through the telling of the story—a collage of responses and reflections from people in Laramie—Matthew would affect the lives of thousands. From a dark and vicious deed, something of value had been rescued.

Exercise: Light a Candle

Write about ways you can light a candle. You can learn from your sorrow and somehow help others to better endure their own. You can grow from the pain you have experienced and share with others what you've learned. Begin by listing those people, things, rituals, events that helped you the most in dealing with your loss:

- the friend who always listened when you called, but never told you what to do
- the grandfather who sent little notes reminding you that he was thinking of you
- your children who helped you realize life went on
- the early morning walks
- dancing to Tina Turner when no one else was around
- the lover who just held you
- the person at the checkout who always asked how you were doing, and meant it

Exercise: What Doesn't Work

Now list those people or things that didn't help:

- the friends who disappeared
- the family member who said, "If I were you . . ."
- the aunt who bent your ear with all of her woes
- drinking too much coffee, wine, beer
- eating all the time
- never eating

Exercise: The Most Valuable Lesson

Think about your lists. What is the most valuable lesson that you learned from the experience? What would you recommend to someone who is faced with a similar challenge? Write for fifteen minutes. This is a difficult exercise when you are in the midst of a loss. It takes distance and perspective. Try to do it. It is one of the most important exercises there is. It removes the what ifs. It helps you understand the transformational power of pain. If you find you can't do it now, come back to it in a few weeks, six months, a year.

CHAPTER 28

You Did It

Once you have experienced the seriousness of your loss, you will be able to

experience the wonder of being alive. It is a fact that once you experience

pain, it sensitizes you to joy.

—ROBERT L. VENINGA

*T*HE CROCUSES HAVE BEGUN THEIR FIGHT AGAINST winter. Morning dawns earlier. The days stretch longer. Alice is home sick, the third day of a bad sinus infection. Today she feels well enough to help me cook a birthday dinner for Paul's dad, who is eighty-three and healthy. As I rush about picking up birthday candles, a chocolate mousse cake, salmon, fresh mint, parsley, basil, arugula, shallots, I tell myself not to view these shopping errands as a burden, but as a sensory experience. I walk through aisles, struck by the beauty of abundance: bins of almonds, pistachios, oats, granola, flour; teeming crates of lettuce, spinach, endive, broccoli, asparagus, peppers, gnarled gingerroot, the smell of cilantro, the voluptuous curves of beets and artichokes.

Spring is coming. I am cooking with Alice. Pablo Neruda's poetry plays in the background. This book is coming to an end. I am happy. I never thought I'd get here. If you had asked me twenty years ago, "Can you ever be happy again?" I would have said, "Katherine will never walk, talk, feed herself. She will be a terrible burden. She has broken my heart. It will never mend. No, I will never be happy."

Last week, Donna and Katherine piled into Donna's van and headed on a road trip to California. Donna wants to visit a couple of her grandchildren, but the main purpose of the trip is to show Katherine the Pacific Ocean and the San Diego Zoo.

Donna calls. "Kat loves the Pacific. We carried her down and sat her where she could put her feet in the water. She laughed and laughed. I took her to Tijuana to visit my granddaughter's in-laws. They had a huge Sunday dinner with chili rellenos, enchiladas, tamales, everything. They loved Kat and were so sweet to her. On the way back, we passed this carnival with lots of lights and music. My granddaughters and I took Kat. She went on the Ferris wheel and the merry-go-round. We're having a wonderful time."

I neaten my desk drawer and come upon a letter from a woman who read *Grief Dancers* and jotted me a note. "Thank you for sharing your story about your daughter. Your words helped me with my disabled daughter. My daughter Jenny is truly a gift from God. Sometimes I think she is an angel unaware." Two decades ago, I would have said I'd rather die than watch Katherine never grow up. Now I embrace that mother's words and know exactly what she means. Angel unaware: Someone placed on this Earth to awaken our hearts and souls. For years I told myself I would lead a full life in spite of Katherine; now I realize how much fuller my life is *because of* Katherine.

In *The Gift of Hope*, Robert Veninga writes, "Love is the ultimate therapy. For when we love, we are transformed. And then we move into a region beyond science. It can be called the spiritual world, the psychic universe, the inner spirit. But call it what you want, it is a world that knows no fear. And harbors no grudge."

Without Katherine, I would not have known, really known, what he was talking about. There are some things we have to experience before they become ours. Loving is one of those things. We can read about it forever, but until we've had our hearts torn open, we don't really understand the concept. Until we've gone through the tough times and found that we love more, not less, because of the struggle, we don't have a clue.

Leslie, an artist in her sixties, says, "When I'm down, I take a walk at night. I look up at the stars and tell myself that what I'm going through has been happening on this Earth for thousands and thousands of years. The stars have seen it all. There's nothing new. Everything has happened many times before. When I get back to my house, I'm calm. I've connected with something much bigger than I am. The stars will keep watching; and it will all be okay."

Sometimes darkness closes in around us. We can barely make it through the day. We tell ourselves to take it one day at a time. It is all we can do. We have no choice. But we have to know, at a very deep level, that things will change. The circumstance might not change—your child may never recover; your marriage may not be salvageable; your sister might die of brain cancer—but how you perceive it will. You will find a strength and tenderness you never thought you had. And you will come to understand that life's sorrows are our greatest teachers. It is through them that we come to know ourselves and what we hold precious. It is through them that we are given the opportunity to create meaning. At the moment we move from asking, "Why me?" to asserting, "Yes, me!" a transformation occurs: We embrace life in its totality; we know the price of love, and we are willing to pay it over and over again. We know the stars will remain in formation. No longer are we afraid.

Alice and I are making an artichoke dip, cold pea-and-mint soup, grilled salmon smothered in an Italian tomato-caper sauce. Alice insisted on bringing out Rita's old china and has set the table with the silver from Paul's grandfather. A bouquet of daffodils sits between the candlesticks. I check my e-mail and find this quote from my dear friend Kate: "Life is a great big canvas; throw all the paint you can on it." Tonight, the fire and candles will be lit, and we will celebrate eighty-three years of a good life. We will toss another bucket on this glorious canvas.

Keep writing. Please keep writing. Be proud of yourself for what you've done. You've created a thing of beauty, your sacred journal. Now keep writing.

"What is REAL?" asked the Rabbit one day. . . . "Does it happen all at once, or bit by bit?"

"It doesn't happen all at once," said the Skin Horse. "You become. It takes a long time. That's why it doesn't often happen to people who break easily, or have sharp edges, or who have to be carefully kept. Generally, by the time you are Real, most of your hair has been loved off, and your eyes drop out and you get loose in the joints and very shabby. But these things don't matter at all, because once you are Real you can't be ugly, except to people who don't understand."

—MARGERY WILLIAMS, *The Velveteen Rabbit*

Recommended Reading

Isabel Allende, *Paula* (New York: HarperCollins Publishers, 1995) In this heart-rending memoir written as her twenty-eight-year-old daughter, Paula, lay in a coma, dying from a rare blood disease, Isabel Allende juxtaposes her personal tragedy against the history of Chile and her family's past. Irony and flights of fantasy mix with the icy reality of Paula's deathly illness. This book is wise, profound, and brilliant.

Isabel Allende, *Aphrodite: A Memoir of the Senses* (New York: HarperCollins Publishers, 1998) An eclectic book that marks Allende's reawakening after the death of Paula, *Aphrodite* is a sensual feast that connects healing to the appreciation of the sensory world. "When my dreams about food began," Allende muses, "I knew that I was reaching the end of a long tunnel of mourning and finally coming out the other end, into the light, with a tremendous desire to eat and cuddle once again."

Warren Bennis, *On Becoming a Leader* (Reading, Mass.: Addison-Wesley Publishing Company, 1994) A leadership book that encourages risk taking, embracing change, learning from adversity, and getting to know oneself in order to be a true leader. Bennis recognizes the power of struggle and loss to shape and strengthen individuals and the importance of writing. "Writing," he says, "is the most profound way of codifying your thoughts, the best way of learning from yourself who you are and what you believe."

Julia Cameron, *The Artist's Way: A Spiritual Path to Higher Creativity* (New York: Jeremy P. Tarcher, 1992) An empowering book for aspiring and working artists, *The Artist's Way* gives suggestions about how to recover your creativity from a variety of "blocks," including limiting beliefs, fear, self-sabotage, jealousy, guilt, addictions, and other inhibiting forces.

Julia Cameron, *The Vein of Gold: A Journey to Your Creative Heart* (New York: Jeremy P. Tarcher, 1996) Once again drawing from her extensive artistic and teaching experience, Cameron presents an ever-widening creative horizon and invites the reader to explore areas such as "the kingdom" of story, sight, sound, relationship, attitude, spirituality, and possibility.

Norman Cousins, *Anatomy of an Illness as Perceived by the Patient: Reflections on Healing and Regeneration* (New York: W. W. Norton & Company, 1979) *Anatomy of an Illness* is a carefully constructed, sober, yet passionate memoir of healing that focuses on the importance of laughter and the will to heal. It is the story of Cousins's recovery from a crippling and supposedly irreversible disease, of a partnership between a physician and patient in beating back the odds, and of the capacity of the human mind and body to regenerate.

Thomas F. Crum, *The Magic of Conflict* (Touchstone Press, 1987) "Conflicts can be disastrous or miraculous," says Crum, "depending upon how you react to them." He provides a set of techniques, including meditation, breathing exercises, openness, and play—Aiki—to lead gently to a reordered state of mind. From overcoming apathy to understanding how conflict doesn't have to mean contest, Crum turns mind–body integration principles into powerful tools.

Clarissa Pinkola Estes, *Women Who Run with the Wolves: Myths and Stories of the Wild Woman Archetype* (New York: Ballantine Books, 1992) Within every woman there lives a powerful force, filled with good instincts, passionate creativity, and ageless knowing. She is the Wild Woman, who represents the instinctual nature of women, and she is an endangered species. Drawing on myths, legends, and fairy tales from a vast and eclectic range of traditions, Estes presents stories to awaken women's strength and creativity and says, "When a secret is not told, grieving goes on anyway, and for life. The keeping of secrets interferes with the natural self-healing hygiene of psyche and spirit. This is one more reason to say our secrets."

Viktor Frankl, *Man's Search for Meaning* (New York: Washington Square Press, 1998) In this profound and moving book Viktor Frankl, a renowned psychiatrist who endured years of unspeakable horrors in Nazi death camps, describes his experience. During, and partly because of, his suffering, Dr. Frankl developed a revolutionary approach to psychotherapy known as logotherapy. Frankl concludes that man's primary motivational force is his search for meaning and purpose in life and says, "It did not really matter what we expected from life, but rather what life expected from us."

Kahlil Gibran, *The Prophet* (New York: Alfred A. Knopf, 1981) A wise man's philosophy on love, marriage, joy and sorrow, time, and friendship, *The Prophet* is a moving and poetic work that explores life's paradox with grace and compassion.

Natalie Goldberg, *Writing Down the Bones: Freeing the Writer Within* (Boston: Shambhala Publications, 1986) An upbeat meditation on writing and a call to write as a way to connect with oneself, Goldberg teaches about letting go and unleashing the writer within.

Natalie Goldberg, *Wild Mind: Living the Writer's Life* (New York: Bantam Books, 1990) Natalie Goldberg gives practical, humorous, thoughtful advice about how to discover your personal style, how to make sentences come alive, and how to overcome procrastination and writer's block. *Wild Mind* also touches on balancing daily responsibilities with a commitment to writing, knowing when to take risks as a writer and human being, and coming to terms with success, failure, and loss, in both life and art.

His Holiness The Dalai Lama and Howard C. Cutler, *The Art of Happiness: A Handbook for Living* (New York: Riverhead Books, 1998) The Dalai Lama offers daily meditations and stories to aid readers in regaining lost happiness in their daily lives. Working with the Dalai Lama, psychiatrist–neurologist Howard Cutler takes a closer look at the psychology of happiness and the blocks that may keep people from it.

Robert A. Johnson, *Inner Work: Using Dreams and Active Imagination for Personal Growth* (New York: HarperSanFrancisco, 1986) Robert Johnson, a Jungian analyst, has written numerous useful books on understanding dream symbols and images. His books are helpful for gaining a better understanding of the meaning and importance of your dreams.

Carl G. Jung and M.-L. Von Franz, *Man and His Symbols* (New York: Doubleday & Company, 1964) Written for the layman, this book is an excellent introduction to Jung's theories of dreams.

Anne Lamott, *Bird by Bird: Some Instructions on Writing and Life* (New York: Doubleday, 1994) A heart-warming, funny book full of writing advice, personal insight, and ideas to get you started writing and keep you going.

Joel Levey and Michelle Levey, *Living in Balance: A Dynamic Approach for Creating Harmony and Wholeness in a Chaotic World* (Conari Press, 1998) Joel and Michelle Levey offer a synthesis of ancient wisdom traditions and cutting-edge research on peak performance to show you how to master the art of attaining balance within an environment of rapid change. Grounded in pragmatic suggestions for finding harmony in love, work, eating, sleeping, exercise, and breathing, the authors suggest ways to stay afloat in your own perfectly balanced ocean regardless of the storms at sea.

Carol S. Pearson, *The Hero Within: Six Archetypes We Live By* (New York: HarperSanFrancisco, 1986) Drawing from literature, anthropology, and psychology, Pearson, a Jungian psychologist, defines six heroic archetypes and shows how we can use these powerful guides to discover our own hidden gifts, solve difficult problems, and transform our lives with rich sources of inner strength.

M. Scott Peck, *The Road Less Traveled: A New Psychology of Love, Traditional Values, and Spiritual Growth* (New York: A Touchstone, 1978) Dr. Peck, a practicing psychiatrist, suggests ways in which confronting and resolving our problems, and suffering through the changes, can enable us to reach a higher level of self-understanding. He discusses the nature of love, relationships, pain, commitment, and religion. On suffering, he says, "One measure—and perhaps the best measure—of a person's greatness is the capacity for suffering. Yet the great are also joyful. This, then, is the paradox."

James W. Pennebaker, *Opening Up: The Healing Power of Expressing Emotions* (New York: The Guilford Press, 1997) Psychologist and professor James Pennebaker has conducted clinical research that sheds new light on the healing value of writing. *Opening Up* interweaves his findings with insightful case studies on keeping secrets, confession, and the hidden price of silence. He explains how writing about problems can improve health, how long-buried trauma affects the immune system, and how it's never too late to heal old emotional wounds.

Sogyal Rinpoche, *The Tibetan Book of Living and Dying* (New York: HarperSanFrancisco, 1993) Based on the *Tibetan Book of the Dead*, *The Tibetan Book of Living and Dying* presents a perennial philosophy of impermanence, goodness, and transformation through suffering. Through anecdotes and stories from religious traditions East and West, Sogyal Rinpoche introduces the reader to the fundamentals of Tibetan Buddhism, moves gradually to the topics of death and dying, and says at one point, "Difficulties and obstacles, if properly understood and used, can often turn out to be an unexpected source of strength."

Sark, *Inspiration Sandwich: Stories to Inspire Our Creative Freedom* (Berkeley, Calif.: Celestial Arts, 1992) A charming, quirky exploration of creativity and the imagination, Sark playfully suggests ways to unleash the fun, creative person inside and to be more alive than ever before.

Wallace E. Stegner, *Where the Bluebird Sings to the Lemonade Springs: Living and Writing in the West* (New York: Random House, 1992) This is a collection of Stegner's essays on writing, friends, his mother, the western landscape, and the ever-changing effect of humanity on it. Particularly excellent are "Letter Much Too Late" and "The Law of Nature and the Dream of Man: Ruminations on the Art of Fiction." Stegner states that "the guts of any significant fiction—or autobiography—is an anguished question."

Steve Van Matre and Bill Weiler, editors, *The Earth Speaks* (Warrenville, Ill.: The Institute for Earth Education, 1983) A beautiful collection of nature images and impressions captured by those who have listened to the earth with their hearts—John Muir, Walt Whitman, Annie Dillard, John Burroughs, Rachel Carson, Aldo Leopold, Edward Abbey, Henry David Thoreau, and many others.

Robert L. Veninga, *A Gift of Hope: How We Survive Our Tragedies* (New York: Ballantine, 1985) Based on the premise that tragedy is a part of life we all must face, *A Gift of Hope* gives thoughtful, caring advice about how to deal with suffering and pain, including the loss of a loved one, heartbreak of a handicapped child, debilitating illness, unwanted divorce, or severe financial setback.

Terry Tempest Williams, *Refuge: An Unnatural History of Family and Place* (New York: Pantheon Books, 1991) In *Refuge*, Terry Tempest Williams weaves together the natural world, the impact of nuclear testing in the Nevada desert, and the loss of her mother, grandmother, and others from cancer. Creative and spiritual, Williams's journal of her mother's death is told through the lens of her own work as a naturalist studying birds in her native Utah.

William Zinsser, *On Writing Well: An Informal Guide to Writing Nonfiction* (New York: Harper & Row, 1976) A guide to writing simply, honestly, carefully, and directly. Zinsser admonishes writers to simplify, fight language clutter, and go for the concrete details.

About the Author

Susan Zimmermann is the author of *Grief Dancers: A Journey into the Depths of the Soul* (1996) and coauthor of *Mosaic of Thought: Teaching Comprehension in a Reader's Workshop* (1997). She speaks throughout the United States on the healing power of writing, the value of our individual stories, and ways to deepen reading and writing experiences for adults and children. A graduate of the University of North Carolina and Yale Law School, she practiced corporate law, then cofounded and served as the executive director of the Public Education and Business Coalition, a nonprofit organization that mobilizes business support for public schools. A lover of the wilderness and believer in the transformative power of the outdoors, she has been a trustee of the Colorado Outward Bound School and is currently the board chair of The Women's Wilderness Institute. Susan lives in the foothills west of Denver with her husband, Paul Phillips, and their four children.